The Fourth Wave

FThe ourth Wave

Business in the 21st Century

Herman Bryant Maynard, Jr.
Susan E. Mehrtens

Berrett-Koehler Publishers
San Francisco

Berrett-Koehler Publishers, Inc.
450 Sansome Street, Suite 1200
San Francisco, CA 94111-3320
Tel: 415-288-0260 Fax: 415-362-2512

ORDERING INFORMATION

Individual sales. Berrett-Koehler publications are available through book-
stores.They can also be ordered direct from Berrett-Koehler at the address
above.

Quantity sales. Special discounts are available on quantity purchases by corporations, associations, and others. For details, contact the "Special Sales
Department" at the Berrett-Koehler address above.

Orders for college textbook/course adoption use. Please contact Berrett-Koehler
Publishers at the address above.

Orders by U.S. trade bookstores and wholesalers. Please contact Publishers
Group West, 4065 Hollis Street, Box 8843, Emeryville, CA 94662.
Tel: 800-788-3123 Fax: 510-658-1834.

Printed in the United States of America
    Printed on acid-free and recycled paper composed of 50%
    recovered fiber, including 10% postconsumer waste.

Library of Congress Cataloging-in-Publication Data
Maynard, Herman Bryant. 1946–
    The fourth wave: business in the 21st century/Herman Bryant Maynard,
Jr., Susan E. Mehrtens. — 1st ed.
    Includes bibliographical references and index.
    p. cm.
    ISBN 1-881052-15-X (hardcover: alk. paper)
    ISBN 1-57675-002-7 (paperback: alk. paper)
    1. Business forecasting. 2.Twenty-first century—Forecasts.
I. Mehrtens, Susan E., 1945– II. Title.
HD30.27.M355 1993   93-2705
338.5'44—dc20   CIP

$18.95

BK

    First Hardcover Printing: May 1993
    First Paperback Printing: August 1996
    00 99 98 97 96   10 9 8 7 6 5 4 3 2 1

This paperback edition contains the complete text of the original hardcover edition.

Cover and book design by Kathryn W. Werhane

Contents

Foreword

IF EVER THE CHINESE CURSE, "May you live in interesting times," has been true, it is during this time of transition for the world. The old tried and true ways are just not working anymore. It seems that when we solve one problem it comes back in a different form, and, what is more, five other problems pop up to take its place.

Technologies that have bettered the lives of a certain proportion of the world's people have emerged from what this book calls the "Second Wave," but they have also led to terrible side effects: three to four hundred species become extinct every day, the destruction of the rain forests is proceeding at a rate that is unthinkable, holes in the ozone layer grow at a rate double the worst predictions, thousands die of starvation every day, and population growth is out of control and exceeds the ability of the planet to support it. Despite all of these dire results of our materialist, growth-oriented system, people in underdeveloped countries around the world say they want the same kind of culture. So the destructive forces feed on themselves. As African scholar and educator Mtombe Mpana puts it, "The American dream has become the world's nightmare."

People in business who get caught in the difficulties of today get into a hopeless state. It is not only that there are societal and global problems. There are difficulties of stress, frustration, anger, fear, and hopelessness at the individual level—coupled with the inner feeling that there is something better, that there is something great for each of us and the planet, and that there is a contribution we can make to getting there. We cannot seem to get a view at a higher level so that we can see the pattern in the seeming contradictions and chaotic events.

Herman Maynard and Susan Mehrtens give us this kind of perspective and more. Like all great creative works, *The Fourth Wave* represents a synergy between seemingly incongruous elements. The authors combine deep corporate and entre-preneurial business experience with a sweeping scholarship in all the disciplines needed to understand the nature of business now and in the future. They hold the hope of what business can be while being brutally realistic about the difficulties experienced today in making the transition. They frame excit-ing concepts with facts about actual changes and anecdotes about what has happened in corporate settings as business-people go through this time of sometimes terrifying change.

I cannot think of a better way to communicate the beauty of this book than to characterize its message as being a heuristic, perhaps a meta-heuristic or a system of heuristics. The typical dictionary definition of the word *heuristic* is that it is a "general-ization or rule of thumb for learning or discovery." It contrasts with *algorithm*, which is a rigid rote law or formula for doing something. Heuristic has the same Greek root as the word *eureka*, which implies the thrill and energy of the moment of creativity. With their story of the transition from the Second Wave to the Third Wave and ultimately to the full effect of the Fourth Wave in the next century, the authors give us many eureka moments, both in the course of reading this book and in the implementation of its ideas. This book's heuristic grounds us in the current realities while showing us a process that will move our work, business, and personal lives into the twenty-first century in a way that is right for each of us and for the planet.

Instead of constricting us like a formula, the heuristic of the Second, Third, and Fourth Waves provides a context within which to turn our difficulties into challenges that we can face with a new faith. Unless we have faith that springs from a deep inner vision for our actions, we will not be able to persist during these difficult times. This book shows us the structure of change so that we know that even setbacks are part of an inevitable process that is leading to a new and better world.

At the same time, Maynard and Mehrtens do not fool us into a complacency, into waiting for this new world to come. They realize that for a variety of reasons, primarily psychological, we find it painful to consider the difficulties of a world in transition and that often the whole subject is avoided as a result. To counteract this, they show us a way to take responsibility with creativity, compassion, and community. They exhort us to live in these times with a vision of what business and the world are and can be that is richer and more textured than anything I have seen written.

Reading this book is like having a wise friend who has gone through the difficulties and opportunities of our time in business and who will take time with great care to make sure that you understand the situation, the process we are going through, and what needs to be done. For some of us, this book lets us know that we are not crazy, that the changes are inevitable, and that we each have a choice as to whether we are going to go through this period into the next century with pain or with exultation. To choose exultation, read and act on this book. Then the old Chinese curse will become a blessing for you.

Michael Ray
John G. McCoy-Banc One Corporation Professor
of Creativity and Innovation and of Marketing,
Graduate School of Business, Stanford University

Preface

TIMES ARE HARD and people are consumed by crises. The challenges posed by political, economic, and environmental problems persist and intensify; there is a decline of genuine leadership in social, political, educational, and religious spheres; unhealthy practices and censorship in business and other institutions continue unabated; and change, a major disruptive force, is omnipresent and accelerating.

Our society, facing momentous challenges in the closing years of the twentieth century, needs visions of the future so attractive, inspiring, and compelling that people will shift from their current mind-set of focusing on immediate crises to one of eagerly anticipating the future—a future where the health and well-being of the earth and its inhabitants is secure.

In this book we create such visions for the world of business. We focus on business for two reasons. First, it is arguably the most powerful institution of our society and the major force affecting world conditions. Second, individual business corporations will survive only if they undergo a major shift to address individual and societal needs and become more democratic in their processes. We present a vision of the current and future role of business in order to foster dialogue in search of positive and proactive responses to the challenges business currently faces.

Over the past five years our respective travel, research, and

networking activities have allowed us to meet some of the
major players and to become part of some of the global groups
operating on the leading edge of business. We have also had
many occasions to talk with people in a wide array of companies
and positions, inside and outside many major corporations.
From these interactions, we have gained a sense of some
disturbing trends occurring in business.

We encountered many indicators of a reality gap, a gap that
exists between where people are and where they see themselves as being. We also noticed a slowing down in movement
from traditional practices toward progressive and enlightened
ways of operating. And we observed wide variance in moods
and attitudes among businesspeople. Some of them, enthusias-
tic and committed, are fired with hope and full of a sense of
promise for the future. Others are full of cynicism, despair,
and fear of reprisal. They stand by passively waiting for the
next shoe to drop.

To counter these trends—to catalyze and support the
debate on the viability of our future and the appropriate role
for business in improving our future prospects, to stimulate
creativity toward building a better world, to help regenerate
a backsliding movement toward more enlightened businesses
and workplaces, to provide a long-term vision of what might
be, and to show how we can achieve that vision—we conceived
the idea of defining a new set of goalposts, which we refer
to as the "Fourth Wave." They reflect leading-edge thinking
on the needed role for business in the world. Our belief
is that this vision of a Fourth Wave will create the tension
needed to pull the more progressive companies forward into a

new era of business leadership and global well-being.

This book is offered as a critique-cum-vision in the hope that it will spark discussion of the reality gap and offer some inducement to getting the hidden and denied conversations out from under the table, to fostering shared truth-telling. Our book is also offered as a map showing how we can travel from our current circumstances to a more promising future. Though some details may seem unrealistic at present, our vision will, we hope, stimulate people's own dreams of what can be. When enough people have dreams, amazing things can be accomplished.

Waves of Change

We have adopted and extended Alvin Toffler's concept of waves of change, introduced in his book *The Third Wave* (1980), to serve as the framework for our vision of business in the twenty-first century. The First Wave of change, the agricultural revolution, has essentially ended and will not be of concern here. The Second Wave, coincidental with industrialization, has covered much of the earth and continues to spread, while a new, postindustrial Third Wave is gathering force in the modern industrial nations. We see a Fourth Wave following close upon the Third.

The Second Wave is rooted in materialism and the supremacy of man. From this orientation flows a stress on competition, self-preservation, and consumption, which has led to such current problems as pollution, solid-waste disposal, crime, family violence, and international terrorism. The Third Wave manifests growing concern for balance and sustainability. As the

Third Wave unfolds, we become more sensitive to the issues of conservation, sanctity of life, and cooperation. By the time of the Fourth Wave, integration of all dimensions of life and responsibility for the whole will have become the central foci of our society. The recognition of the identity of all living systems will give rise to new ways of relating and interacting that nourish both humans and nonhumans.

Each wave has a distinctive worldview, epitomized as:

Second Wave—We are separate and must compete.

Third Wave—We are connected and must cooperate.

Fourth Wave—We are one and choose to cocreate.

We begin our book by identifying trends that reflect fundamental changes in our worldview and underlie the emergence of a Fourth Wave. In the chapters that follow we characterize the central thrust of the Second, Third, and Fourth Waves for seven key areas of business. Our intent is not to be exhaustive, nor to document all that is happening, but to sketch in persuasive—and provocative—fashion the broad outlines of a vision of how today's realities can be transformed into a new era of business leadership and global well-being.

A Vision of the Future Out of the Future

Our book is based on recognizing the real nature of our current predicament: we do not need "more of the same" but something new. So we have to intentionally separate ourselves from the strictures and limitations of the past and create a vision of the future out of the future. As a result, our book offers a unique, unprecedented vision of what lies ahead for our society, for our corporations, and for us as individuals.

People need a vision of a positive, desirable reality over the edge of the horizon toward which they can grow. Therein lies hope and personal empowerment.

Acknowledgments

This book has its antecedent in a monograph we coauthored in 1990, titled "Moving Toward the Millennium: The Corporation in the Twenty-First Century." Steven Piersanti, our publisher, and other friends believed that our views and way of expressing them could make a difference and pushed us to step up to the challenge of turning the monograph into a book.

A work that stretches the boundaries of what we define as "real" necessarily draws on the ideas and support of many people. Sometimes this happens through direct interaction and sometimes indirectly through writings and oral histories. To the many people who have shared with us their ideas on what is happening in business and in the world, we are both grateful and indebted. The bibliography lists many of the authors on whose thinking we drew heavily for our ideas on global trends.

We would like to thank our colleagues in the World Business Academy, especially Willis Harman and John Hormann, for providing us with opportunities to collect data and ideas over the last several years.

We are especially grateful to Christine Maynard and Pauline Mehrtens for their support, both tangible and intangible, in the early stages of this project. We are grateful also for their insightful suggestions on better ways to phrase the concepts here, which made this work vastly better than it might otherwise have been.

To our publisher, Steven Piersanti, and our editor, Alis Valencia, must go a big thanks for their unwavering support, extraordinary interest, and personal commitment to this project.

We are also grateful to the people who reviewed the manuscript before publication and especially want to thank Keith Darcy and Meg Wheatley.

To our many friends who gave us encouragement, support, hospitality, and nourishment, a heartfelt "thank you."

Herman Bryant Maynard, Jr.
Littleton, Colorado

Susan E. Mehrtens
Mineola, New York

February 1993

The Authors

Herman Bryant Maynard, Jr., is an international consultant on personal and organizational transformation and a licensed Master for delivery of "Avatar" (Star's Edge International), a course designed to assist individuals in taking conscious command of their lives.

His specialties include business turnarounds and transformation of business cultures. Now a member of the growing international network of businesspersons and consultants who are pioneering a new business paradigm, Maynard serves on the board of directors for the World Business Academy, the World Trust, and the International Center for Organizational Design. He has been co-chairman of the National Learning Foundation and a guest speaker at the Stanford Business School, and he spent twenty-two years with Du Pont, holding a number of professional and managerial positions in manufacturing, research, marketing, sales, product management, new business development, and administration.

Maynard's educational background includes a bachelor's degree in chemical engineering as well as numerous courses and seminars in marketing, management, and the development of personal and intuitive skills applicable to business. He is a contributing author to *New Traditions in Business* and *The New Paradigm in Business*.

Susan E. Mehrtens is president of The Potlatch Group
Inc., a research organization specializing in the analysis of
business trends related to global evolution and social change.
Since establishing the business in 1987, she has undertaken a
wide variety of research projects for clients that range from the
Fortune 500 (AT&T, Du Pont, General Motors, Sears) to
smaller businesses, schools, and private foundations, such as
the Institute of Noetic Sciences, World Business Academy,
International Management Institute, Saybrook Institute, and
Schweisfurth Foundation.

After receiving her Ph.D. from Yale University, Mehrtens
taught at Queens College, City University of New York, and
the College of the Atlantic in Bar Harbor, Maine, in the fields
of environmental studies, marine studies, medieval studies, history, Latin, and Greek.

She is the coauthor of an ecology text, *Earthkeeping*; the
editor of *Revisioning Science*, a festschrift dedicated to Willis W.
Harman; and coauthor of a forthcoming book on current market
trends, *What's Going On?*

EXECUTIVE SUMMARY

Toward a New Business Era

OUR SOCIETY, facing momentous challenges in the closing years of the twentieth century, needs visions of the future so attractive, inspiring, and compelling that people will shift from their current mind-set of focusing on immediate crises to one of eagerly anticipating the future—a future where the health and well-being of the earth and its inhabitants is secure.

In this book we create such visions for the world of business. We focus on business for two reasons. First, it is arguably the most powerful institution of our society and the major force affecting world conditions. Second, individual business corporations will survive only if they undergo a major shift to address individual and societal needs and become more democratic in their processes. We present a vision of the current and future role of business in order to foster dialogue in search of positive and proactive responses to the challenges business currently faces.

Hallmarks of a Changing World

To meet the challenges posed by a world that is changing at an ever-increasing pace, we must become acquainted with the changes that are occurring. We have identified seven trends that we believe underlie the emergence of a new worldview.

Shift in Consciousness

Increasing numbers of people around the world are concluding that consciousness is primary, that the mind or spirit has a reality comparable to material objects (Harman 1988; Renesch 1991; Cook 1991; Rothschild 1991). In reexamining the assumptions, values, and directions of their lives, people increasingly see themselves as the creators of their realities. They place emphasis on interconnectedness and wholeness—of everyone and everything—and affirm the central role of inner wisdom and inner authority (Harman 1988, 1992). More often than not, they are committing themselves to make a difference in the world.

The shift in consciousness is more than just rapid and profoundly challenging; it is paradigmatic, representing a fundamental change that calls into question our entire worldview and all the conscious and unconscious assumptions on which that worldview rests. Each of the remaining trends we identify is a natural companion to or consequence of this shift in consciousness.

Disenchantment with Scientism

There is a growing disenchantment with scientism, the tendency to reduce all reality and experience to mathematical descriptions of physical and chemical phenomena. Since the time of Descartes, we in the West have stressed rational truth: it has been widely accepted that science and scientific processes are the way to determine truth and that rational intelligence and logical thought are the most valuable abilities we have. But these attitudes are now being questioned in the light of growing evidence that there are many experiences and events that cannot be explained if what is "real" is only that which can be touched or measured (Harman 1988).

Inner Sources of Authority and Power

The growing credence accorded those processes and experiences we cannot explain or measure is reflected in an increased reliance by many people on an inner source of authority and power, "unconscious knowing" (Harman 1988). This unconscious knowing is revealed to us through such familiar experiences as inspiration, creativity, revelation, and intuition; for some people it may be communicated through a higher self or inner self-helper (Damgaard 1987; Speck 1935).

The new appreciation of "authority from within" is being reflected in the desire of many persons to live and work to their full capacity. People are exhibiting increasing reluctance to have others make their decisions for them or to determine how they are to live and work. This is fomenting revolution in the workplace (Rifkin 1992; Stroh, Reilly & Brett 1990; "The Battle for Control" 1992) and in the global political landscape.

Respiritualization of Society

Many in the Western world are responding to the lack of a sense of balance, purpose, and personal power by bringing spirituality into their lives and work (Harman 1988; Harman & Hormann 1990). People are increasingly engaged in a search for such things as meaning, purpose, inner authority and peace, truth, love, compassion, self-worth, dignity, wisdom, a higher power, and a sense of unity with others—and the means to express them.

Decline of Materialism

We have begun to see a basic reorientation of values (e.g., Strom 1992a,c; Rose 1990; Harman 1982; Schwartz & Ogilvy 1979; Norton 1991) manifest, for instance, in global politics as shifts from competition to cooperation. Other such value shifts are from exploitation to caring, from materialism to spirituality, and from consumerism to a concern for social and economic justice. Greed has become less acceptable; there is a movement away from materialism toward intangibles such as honesty, truth, courage, conviction, self-worth, the quality of relationships, and personal fulfillment.

Political and Economic Democratization

The rising up of oppressed peoples of the world to demand greater political democratization is a global trend well documented by the media. Less well known are the campaigns by partisans of the New International Economic Order (NIEO), which calls for new value systems, stressing in particular environmental sustainability and economic justice. This viewpoint argues for responsible accounting for environmental resources such as air, water, and soil (Ekins 1986b) and an end to economic imperialism, the domination of global economic activities by the Western powers (George 1986). It also stresses the need to recognize the reality of global interdependence.

Beyond Nationality

Many analysts and social commentators see our civilization evolving into a world beyond nationality (Pollack 1992;

Blumenthal & Chace 1992; "The Battle for Control" 1992; Gelb 1991; Wright 1992). Nation states, including many defined solely on ethnic and linguistic grounds, will form regional groupings linked together economically and technologically in an interdependent, "borderless world" (Ohmae 1990).

Bioregionalism is emerging as the guiding concept for such regional groupings (see, for example, McHugh 1992). In this view, the Earth is divided into ecologically unified areas sharing habitat, soil, climate, and faunal similarities (Sale 1986; Anderson 1986).

The trends toward economic democratization and global interdependence remind us that globalization is more than merely putting a factory in each major region of the world or shifting corporate loyalty away from a particular country or tackling global problems such as acid rain and technology transfer. Globalization comes down to facing the challenge of reworking our contemporary value system, which assumes that information is proprietary; that bigger is better; that material growth leads to happiness; that the world is one vast "global shopping center" and the Earth a "gigantic toolshed" (a phrase coined by Clarence Glacken [Ehrenfeld 1978, 177]); and that central planning, efficiency, and the rationalization of power are natural and appropriate, regardless of locale or culture.

Emergence of the Fourth Wave

We have adopted and extended Alvin Toffler's concept of waves of change, introduced in his book *The Third Wave* (1980), to serve as the framework for our vision of business in the twenty-first century. The First Wave of change, the agricultural revolution, has essentially ended and will not be of concern here. The Second Wave, coincidental with industrialization, has covered much of the Earth and continues to spread, while a new, postindustrial Third Wave is gathering force in the modern industrial nations. We see a Fourth Wave following close upon the Third.

The Second Wave is rooted in materialism and the supremacy of man. From this orientation flows a stress on competition, self-preservation, and consumption, which has led to such current problems as pollution, solid-waste disposal, crime, family violence, and international terrorism. The Third Wave manifests growing concern for balance and sustainability. As the Third Wave unfolds, we become more sensitive to the issues of conservation, sanctity of life, and cooperation. By the time of the Fourth Wave, integration of all dimensions of life and responsibility for the whole will have become the central foci of our society. The recognition of the identity of all living systems will give rise to new ways of relating and interacting that nourish both humans and nonhumans.

Each wave has a distinctive worldview, epitomized as:

Second Wave—We are separate and must compete.

Third Wave—We are connected and must cooperate.

Fourth Wave—We are one and choose to cocreate.

A New Role for Business: Global Stewardship

The business of business is not only business. In recent decades, business has emerged as the dominant institution in global culture (Hawken 1992). The other institutions of society—political, educational, religious, social—have a decreasing ability to offer effective leadership: their resources limited, their following fragmented, their legitimacy increasingly questioned, politicians, academics, priests, and proselytizers have neither the resources nor the flexibility to mount an effective response to the manifold challenges we are facing. Business, by default, must begin to assume responsibility for the whole.

Most corporations today are Second Wave, centralized and hierarchical, focused on values like profit, efficiency, bigness, and growth. The Second Wave's derivation lay in the army model, even its language and goals reflecting this military origin: survival, self-preservation, beating the competition, winning. Success is measured by the bottom line, the generation of profits, and long-term time horizons are defined as five to ten years.

The range of corporate activities is narrowly confined to business and things economic and technological, and CEOs are accountable only to their stockholders. Corporate attitudes and policies reflect nationalistic concerns, and globalization is regarded as a process of economic investment in foreign countries. Business is viewed as a way to make a living.

Now business is being pressured to become a more responsible and more multipurpose institution. Its original purpose of generating profits through the production and distribution of goods and services must continue for the company to survive, but in Third Wave society, business is also coming to be regarded as the producer of moral effects (Forest 1991), the creator of much more than a financial bottom line.

The transition between the Second and Third Waves entails

the corporation coming to see itself as a creator of value. Its philosophy of doing business undergoes a profound shift as it focuses more on serving the needs of its various stakeholders (now defined as all parties who have a relationship to the firm, not just its owners) than on production per se. This is done in the belief that if the corporation serves the customer, employee, and community, then the customer, employee, and community will serve it (Bennett 1991; Norton 1991). Strategic thinking is reoriented to anticipate future needs independent of the corporation, and business is increasingly regarded as a vehicle through which people can grow and serve others.

A host of new questions epitomizes the shift from Second to Third Waves: The old "Are we making money?" becomes "Are we creating value?" "Are we beating the competition?" shifts to "Do we understand the need?" "Are we gaining market share?" emerges as "Are we providing the right level and kind of service?" Asking such new questions and doing business in the Third Wave mode requires a basic shift of consciousness away from fear toward trust, away from the need for control toward giving up control, away from rigidity toward a learning culture.

The Fourth Wave corporation will recognize its role as one of stewardship for the whole in addition to providing goods and services to a particular customer base. It will have shifted its self-image from that of a primarily manufacturing to a primarily serving organization (Harman 1982) and will act as a leader in addressing global issues, focusing on what is best for all. The model of servant leadership originated by Robert K. Greenleaf (see, for example, Kiechel 1992) will become the corporate ethos of the Fourth Wave.

Business can take a leadership position in global responsibility and citizenship by doing the following:

Make the intellectual shift from wanting to beat the competition to wanting to serve the world.

Set as its primary focus the identification of needs—as the citizens of the world define these for themselves.

Recognize and capitalize on the advantages of a global organization committed to stewardship: its transnational character, its diversity of personnel, its wealth of global interests and distribution channels.

Recognize that the organization is a composite of the individual people within and appended to its structure.

Think globally while acting locally.

Corporate Wealth Redefined

As corporations move in new directions, they will need to find new ways to define wealth. Alternative economists have created a variety of techniques for social accounting (Leipert 1986). These include the following:

Universalization of capital ownership, which is not as radical an idea as it may seem when one considers the near universality of stock ownership represented by the holdings of pension fund systems.

Internalization of the social and environmental costs of doing business, which are currently treated as externalities.

Capitalization of natural resources with the creation of pollution credits that savvy companies such as 3M are already turning into saleable assets.

9

Resource accounting, a new form of capital accounting at the macroeconomic level (Ekins 1986b), has been designed to ensure that our resource bases are not destroyed. It strives to describe such things as the state of the resource base, the depreciation of natural assets, the depreciation of manufactured assets (the infrastructure), the use of human resources, and the maintenance or deterioration of human health.

In addition, progressive business analysts are identifying new forms of wealth, such as intellectual capital, creativity, and intrapreneurship. All of these forms of wealth depend on people (Wriston 1990).

In the Second Wave corporation, wealth derives from creating a positive bottom line while satisfying employees and making a good impression on consumers. It is profit-driven, with little incentive to consider social accounting and other such reforms.

The Third Wave corporation will be more supportive of social and resource accounting as it begins to change its underlying value system.

Fourth Wave business will have a wider agenda, reflecting its leadership role and its acceptance of responsibility for the whole. It will ask, "What are we doing to improve the health of the planet?" Social and resource accounting will be the convention, and ownership of business will be universalized in the communitarian ethos then prevailing.

Seeing the corporation in this Fourth Wave way has significant implications for its internal structure and governance.

Evolving Forms of Corporate Structure

It is becoming clear that new organizational structures are needed for corporations to flourish in the future. Current critics of corporate structure note that the Second Wave model, characterized by hierarchy and an authoritarian form of management, is inflexible, leaving organizations unable to respond quickly to change. It disempowers people and fosters divisiveness, double agendas, and destructive conflicts. A variant of the traditional hierarchy, the matrixed organization, divides employee loyalties and thus splits the decision-making process, creating inefficiencies and low levels of trust.

There is no incentive in a Second Wave corporation for a manager to abandon the traditional role, which insists that he or she is in charge. Given the information revolution in the last ten years, this image is as outdated as it is destructive. Rather than continue the illusion that knowledge and wisdom reside in management alone, managers must come to see the corporation as a learning organization for all levels of employees, including themselves (O'Toole 1985; Naisbitt 1984; Senge 1990).

More effective today than the matrix model is the business unit model. Although still Second Wave, the business unit model affords the benefits of autonomy, unified loyalties, single focus (the recognition of and response to market need), and flexibility. Businesses such as General Electric that have shifted toward the business unit structure are flourishing. Those stuck in the centralized or matrixed structure seem likely to face implosion (collapse into themselves).

One way out of the current corporate dilemma threatening implosion is to create an environment in which people feel safe and supported. Such an environment fosters true diversity; that is, it recognizes and appreciates the differences of employee styles and experiences, as well as differences of race and gender. The creative, imaginative oddball is valued as much as the conventional worker. Creating a safe environment also entails the establishment of a clear priority of tolerating each other's frailties and needs.

We envision the Third Wave corporation moving into the team-value model, which is driven by the desire to create value. Functioning in an environment of truth-telling and integrity, business under the team-value model is undertaken collaboratively with coworkers and customers. It is also democratic, with everyone on the team being equal. Managers are elected by members of the team to serve as an interface with other groups. Like the business unit in its autonomy, the team-value organizational model also shares the advantages of flexibility and responsiveness to changing market needs and trends.

The corporation of the Fourth Wave will be structured according to a community model. Because the Fourth Wave in general will occur after a shift in global consciousness, it will manifest many features that seem unrealistic to us today; for example, the devaluation of money as the primary motivator, the absence of hierarchy, and the elimination of external employee evaluation. Like the Third Wave model, the corporation-in-community will be democratic, participatory, and focused on the customer. It will further be driven by a shared vision and will likely operate as much by intuitive processes and techniques as by the logical and rational methods we find familiar today.

The Corporation as Community

The long-term health and prosperity of the contemporary corporation depends on more than its response to globalization or reform of its governance and structure. An equally important factor is how the corporation chooses to respond to the demands of its community.

In acting locally, the corporation functions as a responsible member of its external community, illustrated, for example, in the current concern for education demonstrated by Xerox corporation or for the environment by Du Pont. The corporation, however, must also come to recognize the need to foster its internal community.

Community is manifested in two ways: as a group of people and as a "way of being" that unites group members. The first type of community is formed by bringing people together in place and time. The second is created when barriers between people are let down (Peck 1987). Under such conditions, people become bonded, sensing they can rely on and trust each other, which produces effective team efforts. When people achieve this feeling of community, their subsequent achievements are nothing short of miraculous.

Second Wave corporations have tended to view community as something external to corporate life. The Third Wave corporation will recognize that it has an internal community, one that extends beyond employees to encompass their families as well. It will deal with employees in a multidimensional way, not simply as cogs in a wheel but as whole persons with emotional, psychological, spiritual, and physical needs;

13

family demands; and personal interests and concerns as valid and as important as the job.

In the longer term future, the close integration of corporate work and family life will be crucial to the success of the corporation (Noble 1992). With feminization of the workplace, corporate leaders will come to realize that prosperity depends on viewing employees in the totality of their humanness as physical, emotional, and spiritual beings. At this point, business will shift into a Fourth Wave perspective, taking a leadership position to ensure the overall health and well-being of its family members.

Fundamental changes in the values that guide how corporations act toward their employees will provide the foundation for building community. Changes that will move corporations from the Second to the Fourth Wave, through a transitional Third Wave, include the following:

Diversity Embraced

The achievement of a truly diverse workplace in racial, ethnic, and sexual terms will produce a profound shift in values and a richer, more diverse set of perspectives about the corporation's customers, goals, performance, and role in the wider society.

Truth and Openness Promoted

An environment of truth—a climate where, in the words of one insightful Du Pont manager, "putting the dirt on the table" is customary and accepted—is necessary for change, healing, and growth, both in individuals and in business. Without an environment where truth is valued, fear becomes pervasive, differing from one situation to the next only in intensity. Resistance to change correlates directly with the level of fear in a given environment. Moreover, without an environment of truth-telling, people fall prey to ethical debasement.

Structural Violence Ended

To be successful in creating a climate of truth and openness, corporations must put an end to structural violence. Structural violence is most commonly seen in the business arena in our management practices. Employees live in fear of being punished, of being intimidated by the boss and shown to be of questionable value to the company or to themselves. Even though blatant punishment is an infrequent occurrence, it does happen, and when it does, it sends a strong message to the remaining people in the organization to beware.

Balance and Moderation Encouraged

The term "addiction" conjures up drug users and alcoholics. But addiction is coming to be more widely defined. Corporate consultants now speak of the corporation itself as an addict and as promoting insidious forms of addiction within its employees (Schaef & Fassel 1988).

How does the corporation do this? The stressors inherent in the tension-riddled matrix organization—arising, for example, from the conflict between business team and functional management's goals—that might drive an employee to drink come immediately to mind, but this is only one way the corporation fosters addiction. Much more problematic is the overt encouragement of workaholism.

Another form of company addiction is the pervasiveness of codependency, or a denial of reality, at all levels of the corporation. Information is filtered, most often unconsciously, so that only partial truths are told. The reporting or discussion of bad

15

news is avoided (the "elephant in the living room" is ignored) because people live in fear of hurting others or of being hurt themselves.

Across the country, in boardroom and bedroom, contemporary Americans are beginning to face the reality of this problem (Fassel 1990; Hawken 1992; Herman & Hillman 1992).

Employee Health and Well-Being Supported

An awareness of the value of the "wellness workplace" (Naisbitt & Aburdene 1985) will move the Second Wave company into sharing responsibility for all-around employee well-being (Third Wave) and then into a leadership position where the corporation includes the goal of employee well-being among its other articulated goals and commits its time and resources to that end (Fourth Wave).

In a wellness workplace, it will be recognized that the cheapest way to handle the costs of medical care is by keeping the staff healthy. Preventive medicine will be the order of the day. Health clubs, recreation centers, and smoking cessation programs (coupled with rigorous nonsmoking policies) will be widely available, provided by the company. For their widely recognized benefits in stress reduction, meditation rooms will be a common feature in every company facility and workers' daily schedules will have meditation breaks, similar to the currently ubiquitous coffee break (Siegel 1985).

Besides being preventive, corporate health care in the future will be holistic, attending to both body and mind.

In its role of fostering community, the corporation will shift to new models of governance, engendering deeper levels of trust, caring, and sharing throughout the internal corporate family. By the time of the Fourth Wave corporation, well into the twenty-first century, the corporation will have taken on a new leadership position in society. Its customers will have been integrated (but not assimilated) into corporate life, and its employees will have reached a level of personal and professional integration such that their lives will have permeable boundaries: people will be able to be the same at work as they are at home. No longer will there be a need for false fronts or the studied reactions so necessary in the codependent corporation of the present. The environment—at home, at work, in the world at large—will be healthy and health supporting.

Ecology and Economics: Toward a Common Cause

Environmentalism is teaching us that we can no longer regard environmental protection as a problem or regard ecology as antagonistic to economics. Rethinking some of the basic assumptions that lie behind the operation of business today presents many opportunities and can offer the proactive businessperson a significant advantage.

That this is not now widely recognized is due in part to ignorance of some basic natural laws:

The growth of natural systems is finite. No matter what the system, be it an individual human body or the global ecosystem, biogeochemical reality tells us that unlimited growth leads to disaster. In the individual, this is called cancer; in the global arena, it is called solid-waste problems and pollution (Murray 1974).

Everything must go somewhere (Commoner 1971). This principle explains why we have our current solid-waste disposal problem: the environment's capacities to absorb more have been exhausted. It is the physical law underlying the necessity of recycling, which is also desirable as a way to conserve valuable natural resources and free us from dependence on dwindling reserves of materials such as oil.

Competition discourages diversity (Murray 1974). The basis for this is the competitive exclusion principle: when species (or businesses) rely on the same limiting resource—when, in other words, they are competing—they cannot coexist indefinitely; one of them will supplant the other over time. In contrast, economists would have us believe that competition encourages diversity and stability.

The law of the retarding lead, or *The dominant species is slow to respond to change.* Ethnologists and ecologists (e.g., Keyes 1983) have noticed that change and creative adaptations to new conditions in the environment tend to be made by individuals who are not dominant in the culture or ecosystem. In terms of business, this means that the new, small start-up entrepreneurial companies or the people working for large corporations who are allowed to be intrapreneurial are likely to be the source of the changes, inventions, and new techniques that permit long-term viability.

Nature knows best and *Everything is connected to everything else* (Commoner 1971). Ignorance of these natural laws by economists has led both to the "tragedy of the commons" and pollution.

Businesspeople can turn these laws to their advantage if they are open to rethinking how business operates. Some twenty years ago, for example, Marshall McLuhan (McLuhan & Powers 1989) suggested how businesspersons could use the competitive exclusion principle to their advantage. McLuhan noted that competition creates resemblance. By that he meant that when companies fall into competition over a market niche, they tend to grow more alike. The longer this process persists, the greater their competition and the harder it becomes for them to gain market share. The way out lies in changing the rules of the game. Savvy businesspeople can use the opportunities sited in environmentalism to do this. Du Pont's decision to opt out of the production of chlorofluorocarbons, constitutes one such example.

Besides providing a competitive edge, environmentalism provides investment opportunities, particularly in the "Sunrise Seven" industries and for companies practicing the "Four Rs." The Sunrise Seven are industries involved in pollution control, recycling and resource substitution, energy efficiency, ecologically tailored energy supply, environmental services, information technology, and biotechnology—all of which have clear wealth-creating potential and long-term viability (Elkington 1986). Businesses that move into the Four Rs—repair, recondition, reuse, and recycle—will flourish as environmental rehabilitation becomes imperative in the Third Wave conservationist era.

By the time of the Fourth Wave, we foresee a shift beyond conservationism, to preservationism, or deep ecology (Devall & Sessions 1985). The deep ecologists call for a fundamental spiritual reawakening on the part of people to the sacred quality of nature. At this point, Earth is likely to be seen as an entity in itself, Gaia, a living being with consciousness. Humans will have come to realize the truth of Buckminster Fuller's dictum, "We are not in control here," and thanks to this humility, we will no longer regard the earth as a "gigantic toolshed."

Our values will be transformed. Contributing one's talents and satisfying higher needs will take precedence over accumulating material possessions. We will work as much to serve the health of the planet and to fulfill our personal purpose as to earn a paycheck. Economic justice and sustainability will be key themes undergirding much of what we do and stand for, both privately and publicly.

Use of Appropriate Technology

Because technology is heavily implicated in our environmental crisis, it is clear that business will have to make significant technological changes to meet the needs of the future. Two cultural trends are encouraging action in this direction.

The first of these is the growing disenchantment with scientism, which denies or disparages nonrational ways of knowing in its stress on the empirical testing of reality (Pascarella 1986). The second trend is the movement for an "appropriate technology" consonant with the laws of ecology and serving to foster sustainability and environmental integrity.

More than just environmental considerations make a technology appropriate (Elkington 1986). Cultural factors must also be considered: population size, educational levels, social structures, the available labor pool, the resource base, market conditions, and infrastructure. Questions of values also arise, since technological development is fraught with moral and philosophical aspects.

This poses a significant challenge for Americans, who generally have an aversion to recognizing the moral content of political discourse, but in the application of technology, it is unavoidable. Contemporary technologies, particularly biotechnologies such as genetic engineering and "algeny," the marriage of biological and robotic technologies (Rifkin 1983), are so powerful and so consequential for the long-term quality of our lives that public articulation of the moral limits of technology is now essential. Some advocates of appropriate technology now call for the institution of social, economic, and political impact statements for new technologies that would resemble the currently required environmental impact statement.

Other challenges also arise. These include educating the public and business in the elements of technology assessment, to obviate the need for issues (and values) to be decided solely by "experts."

Developing review procedures and public education programs relates to another challenge: intentionality. We are long past the time in our evolution when we can continue to act without awareness of just what it is we are doing. We must, in short, begin to act intentionally. Unfortunately, most people live their lives in unconscious repetition of deeply ingrained habits. Learning to live intentionally will most likely happen in the context of the Fourth Wave corporation.

In the face of the rising societal awareness of the importance of ethics, the corporation faces the challenge to institutionalize

21

the process of ethical decision making. Some companies are creating a position of corporate ethicist, an employee whose charge is to analyze the boundary conditions and strategic constraints on the corporation in the light of environmental, technological, political, societal, and economic factors.

By the time of the Fourth Wave, technology will reflect a collaborative and ecological ethos. Fourth Wave people's attitudes about information and the power it represents will be very different from ours. Power will lie within each person, so transfer of information is likely to be freer and may occur in forms much faster than anything we can conceive of today.

Leadership in the Era of Biopolitics

Our world is moving quickly into the biopolitical era, thanks to recent advances in biotechnology, the environmental crisis, and global democratization. As we make the transition to this new era, corporate leaders will accept new roles and take on new responsibilities.

Biopolitics, the politics of the future, will deal with our ability to produce change in living systems. In contrast to politics, which encompasses nations and gradual evolutionary change, biopolitics will encompass the whole Earth, or the biosphere, and exponential rates of change.

Another difference from conventional politics will be the "collapse of privatism" (Anderson 1987, 361). The traditional distinction between public and private will become blurred because private values will be recognized as extremely consequential to public welfare. In the biopolitical environment, no one will be able to claim he or she is apolitical. We all breathe

the air, we all live in an ecosystem; therefore, we are all inextricably part of the political process.

The central player on the global biopolitical scene will be business, since it will have institutionalized a concern for environmental preservation. Leaders in business will become de facto leaders of biopolitics, and in this dual capacity, such men and women will need a host of personal and professional qualities.

Chief among these will be personal maturity. At a time when the corporation will have emerged from codependency and unconsciousness, its leaders will necessarily have done likewise. This will be manifested in a level of consciousness that enables each leader to be aware of his or her conscious and unconscious mind. No longer living in self-deception, these leaders will be capable of clear thinking and effective action. They will have learned to control their innate urge for omnipotence.

Equally important, the leaders of Fourth Wave business will be ethically sensitive, in touch with the feminine as well as the masculine in themselves, and supportive of the reorientation of values that the feminine represents. In this as in other ways, the heads of business will not be able to ignore their role as moral leaders.

With these attributes, Fourth Wave biopoliticians will address some awesome tasks. They will influence public dialogue while fostering the integration of economic, environmental, technological, and social problems. To a large extent, they will define the future direction for the evolution of the Earth. They will do this amid a society facing the challenge of living on the slope of a steep learning curve (Anderson 1987), where change is rapid and disorientation a constant threat. As learning organizations, corporations will help move society along this curve, their leaders serving as role models for our adaptation and maturation into Fourth Wave civilization.

Business in the Twenty-First Century

Consider the following visions of the new corporation:

As an exemplar for other institutions in society.

As a global citizen acting locally, while thinking globally.

As an advocate of the living economy, practicing social and resource accounting.

As an organization committed to serve, aware of its identity as a producer of moral effects.

As a community of wellness, aware of the full range of its corporate stakeholders.

As a model of environmental concern.

As a pioneer in appropriate technologies, skilled in technology assessment.

As an organization led by biopoliticians who are fully aware of their responsibility to realize the destiny of modern men and women.

This work is offered as a critique-cum-vision in the hope that it will spark discussion of the reality gap and offer some inducement to shared truth-telling. Business success in the next millennium will require moving into a new game that has already begun. Given correct information and time to wrestle with the issues, our businesses and our society will make constructive decisions. But we must all take care lest, by operating out of fear or an "I have the answer" attitude, we lock ourselves into repeating mistakes of the past.

HALLMARKS OF CHANGE

Shift in Consciousness

Disenchantment with Scientism

New (Inner) Sources of Authority and Power

Respiritualization of Society

Decline in Materialism

Spreading Political and Economic Democratization

Movement Beyond Nationality

ONE

Hallmarks of a Changing World

To MEET THE CHALLENGES posed by a world that is changing at an ever-increasing pace, we must let go of values, beliefs, and practices that have or shortly will become anachronistic and reformulate new ones that are congruent with changed circumstances. The first step in this process is to become acquainted with the changes that are occurring. Because change is omnipresent, it is especially important to identify those trends that promise transformative change. In this chapter we describe seven trends that we believe underlie the emergence of a new worldview.

Shift in Consciousness

Increasing numbers of people around the world are concluding that consciousness is primary, that the mind or spirit has a reality comparable to material objects (Harman 1988; Renesch 1991; Cook 1991; Rothschild 1991). Many have had transformative experiences (life-changing dreams, journeys inward that reveal new vistas, near-death experiences, series of intuitive knowings [Porter, n.d.]) that have led them to realize they are more than their physical body and logical mind—that there are levels of reality beyond what can be seen, touched, tasted, and smelled.

In reexamining the assumptions, values, and directions of their lives, people are beginning to see themselves as the creators of their realities. They are placing emphasis on interconnectedness and wholeness—of everyone and everything —and affirming the central role of inner wisdom and inner authority (Harman 1988, 1992). More often than not, they are committing themselves to make a difference in the world.

Our discussions with successful people in business, coupled with a study of scientific and contemporary literature, affirm that this global shift in consciousness is not mere New Age hype but the expression of a new worldview. For example, Nobel Prize-winning scientists Roger Sperry (1978), Sir John Eccles (Eccles & Popper 1977), Eugene Wigner (1967, 1982), Sir Arthur Eddington (1929), James Jeans (1943), and Brian Josephson (1985) have all concluded that a worldview based on consciousness emerging from matter (the brain) does not account for all that we see and experience. Such noted business consultants and futurists as George Land, Robert Theobald, and Willis Harman have discussed this in large public forums. It is on the lips of political figures such as Václav Havel, who, standing before the United States Congress as president of Czechoslovakia, reminded us that "consciousness is primary" (Havel 1990, 37). And there is even talk among sober, sensible businesspersons of a global mind change occurring in the world (Rose 1990).

The shift in consciousness is more than just rapid and profoundly challenging; it is paradigmatic, representing a fundamental change that calls into question our entire world-view and all the conscious and unconscious assumptions on which that worldview rests. Each of the remaining trends we identify is a natural companion to or consequence of this shift in consciousness.

Disenchantment with Scientism

There is a growing disenchantment with scientism, the tendency to reduce all reality and experience to mathematical descriptions of physical and chemical phenomena. From this perspective, a Beethoven sonata would be described by focus-ing on the constituent parts (cats' guts, horses' tails, wood, metal, rubber, felt) of the musical instruments involved, the amplitudes and frequencies of the sound waves produced, and the mechanisms of auditory perception (ear, brain). This, how-ever, gives us little, if any, sense of the feeling quality of the experience of listening to beautiful music.

Since the time of Descartes, we in the West have stressed rational truth: it has been widely accepted that science and scientific processes are the way to determine truth and that rational intelligence and logical thought are the most valuable abilities we have. But these attitudes are now being questioned in the light of growing evidence that there are many expe-riences and events that cannot be explained if what is "real" is only that which can be touched or measured (Harman 1988). It is increasingly accepted that such phenomena as feelings and intuition expand the range of human potential to find answers ("Seize the Future" 1990), making both rational and nonrational processes legitimate components in the search for knowledge and understanding.

Inner Sources of Authority and Power

The growing credence accorded those processes and experiences we cannot explain or measure is reflected in an increased reliance by many people on an inner source of authority and power, "unconscious knowing" (Harman 1988). This unconscious knowing is revealed to us through such familiar experiences as inspiration, creativity, revelation, and intuition; for some people it may be communicated through a higher self or inner self-helper (Damgaard 1987; Speck 1935).

This new appreciation of "authority from within" is being reflected in the desire of many persons to live and work to their full capacity. People are exhibiting increasing reluctance to have others make their decisions for them or to determine how they are to live and work. And increasing numbers are waking up to the fact that they can give legitimacy to or withhold it from the various institutions of society (Burton 1990; Natale & Wilson 1990; Kelly 1992). For instance, environmentally destructive practices by both corporations and governments are coming to be regarded by the public as irresponsible and therefore illegitimate and intolerable.

Recognition that power and authority lie in the hands of individuals, not institutions, is fomenting revolution in the workplace (Rifkin 1992; Stroh, Reilly & Brett 1990; "The

Table 1. Hallmarks of a changing world

Shift in Consciousness
Consciousness is primary: we create our realities and seek wholeness.

Disenchantment with Scientism
Intuition and other nonrational processes complement reason in the search for knowledge and understanding.

New (Inner) Sources of Authority and Power
We decide ourselves how we live and work and take steps to ensure that our institutions serve us.

Respiritualization of Society
We are engaged in a search for meaning, purpose, truth, love, compassion, self-worth, wisdom, and unity—and the means to express them.

Decline in Materialism
Intangibles such as honesty, openness, courage, conviction, personal fulfillment, caring, cooperation, and justice are the dominant forces guiding our actions.

Spreading Political and Economic Democratization
No room is left for political or economic imperialism.

Movement Beyond Nationality
Global interdependence is unavoidable.

Battle for Control" 1992) and in the global political landscape. Democratic processes are being adopted in growing numbers of workplaces, and in the past several years oppressed peoples of the world have been successfully demanding representational processes and self-determination.

Respiritualization of Society

Many in the Western world are responding to the lack of a sense of balance, purpose, and personal power by bringing spirituality into their lives and work (Harman 1988; Harman & Hormann 1990). People are increasingly engaged in a search for such things as meaning, purpose, inner authority and peace, truth, love, compassion, self-worth, dignity, wisdom, a higher power, and a sense of unity with others—and the means to express them.

This respiritualization of society is manifested in various forms, including participation in traditional religious forums (Western and Eastern), New Age pursuits, self-designed modes of personal quest (meditation, for example), and spreading efforts to incorporate spiritual values in the workplace (Autry 1991; Miller 1992; Orsborn 1992).

As matters spiritual return to respectability in our culture, we see a revival of the value once accorded to intuition (Kelly 1992; Pascarella 1986), thus adding to the growing practice of combining intuitive knowledge and traditional analytical skills.

Decline of Materialism

We have begun to see a basic reorientation of values (e.g., Strom 1992a,c; Rose 1990; Harman 1982; Schwartz & Ogilvy

1979; Norton 1991) manifest, for instance, in global politics as shifts from competition to cooperation. Other such value shifts are from exploitation to caring, from materialism to spirituality, and from consumerism to a concern for social and economic justice. Greed has become less acceptable; there is a movement away from materialism toward intangibles such as honesty, truth, courage, conviction, self-worth, the quality of relationships, and personal fulfillment.

Directly allied to these value shifts is the redefinition of business (Norton 1991; Morin 1992). Once seen as a way to make a living or a way to get rich, business is increasingly viewed as a vehicle through which individuals can realize their personal vision, serve others and the planet, and make a difference in the world. People are saying they do not want to work just to make money; they want to create value. And they want to create this value in an environment that meets their needs and gives them something to feel proud of. This means that how the corporation acts matters. Workers want the values of the corporation and the corporation's leaders to be such that they can identify with the corporation and share its commitments.

Political and Economic Democratization

The rising up of oppressed peoples of the world, East, West, and South, to demand greater political democratization is a global trend well documented by the media in the past several years. Less well known are the campaigns by partisans of the New International Economic Order (NIEO), which are representative of the growing worldwide push for economic democratization (cf. Daly 1973a,b; Henderson 1976, 1978, 1981; Schumacher 1973b, 1978b).

The NIEO, composed mostly of Third World figures and Western alternative economic theorists, calls for new value systems, stressing in particular environmental sustainability and economic justice. This viewpoint argues for responsible accounting for environmental resources such as air, water, and soil (Ekins 1986).

Also stressed in this view is the need to create appropriate technologies, fitted to the cultural level and needs of the people and locale, rather than the massive importation of Western high-tech processes and devices. Recognizing that their countries are rich in human resources and poor in monetary buying power, many spokespersons for the NIEO seek to shift economic activity away from its current focus on materials toward more labor-intensive or information-intensive procedures.

To foster economic justice, NIEO advocates call for an end to economic imperialism, the domination of global economic activities by the Western powers (George 1986), and for the recognition of the reality of global interdependence. Regarding information as a form of power, NIEO rhetoric speaks much of the free exchange of information, presenting a clear challenge to contemporary notions of information as proprietary.

Beyond Nationality

Many analysts and social commentators see our civilization evolving into a world beyond nationality (Pollack 1992; Blumenthal & Chace 1992; "The Battle for Control" 1992;

Gelb 1991; Wright 1992). Nation states, including many defined solely on ethnic and linguistic grounds, will form regional groupings linked together economically and technologically in an interdependent, "borderless world" (Ohmae 1990).

Bioregionalism is emerging as the guiding concept for such regional groupings (see, for example, McHugh 1992). In this view, the Earth is divided into ecologically unified areas sharing habitat, soil, climate, and faunal similarities (Sale 1986; Anderson 1986).

Such intergovernmental organizations as the Arab League, the Organization of African Unity, and the Organization of Economic Cooperation and Government and non-governmental organizations (NGOs) like The Other Economic Summit (TOES) are harbingers of this borderless world. So are charitable, quasipolitical, and juridical units such as the World Health Organization, International Red Cross, the World Bank, and the World Court. Organizations of these sorts will continue to proliferate and play an increasingly important role in contemporary life (Lewis 1992).

The trends toward economic democratization and global interdependence remind us that globalization is more than merely putting a factory in each major region of the world. It is more than shifting corporate loyalty away from a particular country or tackling global problems such as acid rain and technology transfer.

Globalization comes down to facing the challenge of reworking our contemporary value system, which assumes that information is proprietary; that bigger is better; that material growth leads to happiness; that the world is one vast "global shopping center" and the Earth a "gigantic toolshed" (after Clarence Glacken, quoted in Ehrenfeld 1978, 177); and that central planning, efficiency, and the rationalization of power are natural and appropriate, regardless of locale or culture. These, and a host of other similar values that we hardly notice, much less question, are being scrutinized and found wanting by many people.

The trends we have described signal the emergence of a fundamentally different worldview. We next explore what this means in terms of how people will think and behave in the Fourth Wave.

WORLDVIEWS

The Second Wave
We are separate and must compete

The Third Wave
We are connected and must cooperate

The Fourth Wave
We are one and choose to cocreate

TWO

Emergence of the Fourth Wave

In HIS BOOK *The Third Wave* Alvin Toffler (1980), introduced the concept of history as a succession of rolling waves of change. This concept holds powerful imagery— a wave building as changes in values, beliefs, and behaviors accumulate and spread in and among societies, cresting as change becomes sufficiently deep and wide to be unstoppable, crashing down to sweep away what lies in front, and then receding with the transformation of society. Waves can collide, representing the conflict of different worldviews. When the newest one prevails, one phase of civilization is replaced by another.

Waves of change can also be viewed from the perspective of an onlooker standing in the water near shore. As a wave builds off in the distance, its beauty and power will be attractive and inspiring. As it comes closer, however, its size and force may become frightening. The observer may either embrace the wave's beauty and power and ride it to shore or attempt to escape its fearsome force and be hammered into the surf or left by the wayside.

Toffler (1980) identified two waves that have swept across civilization—the First Wave, the spread of agriculture, and the Second Wave, industrialization—and characterized a new, postindustrial Third Wave that is currently gathering force among modern industrial nations. The confluence of the Second and Third Waves means that we now live with two different worldviews—one increasingly recognized as out-dated (Second Wave) and another just beginning to be realized (Third Wave). The traditional, culturally approved way of viewing reality is being reevaluated, presenting us with a multi-faceted challenge to the values and priorities of our Second Wave culture. This has engendered turmoil, tensions, and distress as those who wish to maintain the status quo come into conflict with those who are committed to radical change.

In time, the ineluctable force of the Third Wave will lead to societal transformation. We believe, however, that this outcome can be hastened by looking ahead to a Fourth Wave, one signaled by the trends we described in Chapter One. The appeal of that Fourth Wave (attractive, yet far enough away to be nonthreatening) is a means to pull people through the resis-tance, struggles, and tough decisions that now impede the flow of the Third Wave.

Worldviews in Transition

The waves of change represent fundamental and pervasive change; no aspect of life is left untouched. Each wave is the manifestation of a distinctive worldview, the values, beliefs, and philosophies that guide how people look at and experience the world around them. To distinguish the worldviews underlying the Second, Third, and Fourth Waves, we focus on those dimensions that can be viewed as providing a foundation for all else.

Relationships and Authority

In the Second Wave, people see themselves as separate from one another and from nature and as needing to compete. The traditional factory, with its focus on mechanization, regimentation, hierarchy, and sales volume, is an expression of these attitudes. It is also a manifestation of peoples' willingness to grant power and authority to others—to accept, in essence, roles as incipient automatons. (For if they did not, such an institutional model is unlikely to have spread throughout our society.)

The consequences of these attitudes are increasingly manifested: environmental degradation due to the irreversible effects of pollution, exhaustion of natural resources, and destruction of ecosystems; serious socioeconomic ills reflected by such realities as huge disparities in income and living standards, rampant crime, joblessness, and poverty; and personal distress manifested in high stress levels, substance abuse, and a general sense of emptiness. In reaction, new Third Wave perspectives of relationships and authority are emerging: people see themselves as connected to one another and to the Earth and consider cooperation, the antithesis of competition, more likely to yield benefits to individuals and society at large. They have a renewed confidence in their own capabilities and are less willing to accept the imposition of authority, preferring to wield the power they now recognize themselves as possessing individually and collectively.

Table 2. Differing worldviews of Second, Third, and Fourth Wave societies

	Second Wave	Third Wave	Fourth Wave
Relation-ships	See ourselves as separate and needing to compete	See ourselves as connected and needing to cooperate	See ourselves as one and choose to cocreate
Authority	Externalized; power seen as outside oneself	Begin to question external authority and retain personal locus of authority, take back power	Manifest collaborative systems where authority is fully internalized; power seen as within the person
Values	Rooted in materialism and the supremacy of man	Manifest growing concern for balance and sustainability	Focused on the integration of life and responsibility for the whole
Security	Seen in material terms	Material foundation questioned	Viewed in terms of personal inner trust
Mode of Inquiry	Stresses linear thinking	Incorporates intuition and nonrational processes	Moves beyond intuition to tap full range of human abilities
Decision Making	Act without awareness from unconscious scripts, rational decision making	Become aware of intentionality and the need for acting with intent	Recognize the centrality of intention

By the time of the Fourth Wave, people will consider themselves as part of a single living system and as sharing a common identity. Authority will be fully internalized, and power will lie within each individual. People will choose to collaborate on creating a future that benefits all living beings, human and nonhuman.

Values and Security

Second Wave values are rooted in materialism and the supremacy of man. People and institutions strive for concrete, external manifestations of achievement, generally measured in terms of monetary value and unlimited in potential magnitude. Financial wealth confers power and a sense of security; those without such wealth are accorded no power or authority and lack security. Moral and ethical values, including such things as honesty and integrity, are subservient to ensuring the means of self-preservation and competitive success.

Third Wave values manifest a growing concern for balance and sustainability. People become more sensitive to the sanctity of life, to the limits on natural resources and hence on growth, and to their unmet spiritual needs. Material gain is but one force driving activity; considerations such as reducing environmental risk, providing service to others, and creating opportunities for personal growth and self-fulfillment become standard variables to enter in the equation. Concomitantly, material wealth assumes less importance. Increasing numbers of people find that intangibles such as dignity, integrity, and inner peace play an important role in gaining a sense of personal validation.

In the Fourth Wave, people will focus on integrating all

dimensions of their life and on undertaking responsibility for the whole. Material gain will not be a sufficient end in itself, nor will it be accorded merit beyond that required to sustain continued function. True wealth will be centered in each individual and manifested as an inner trust—an awareness of and belief in the fullness of one's being.

Modes of Inquiry and Decision Making

All forms of Second Wave inquiry stress linear thinking, logical, step-by-step progress from one discovery or conclusion to the next. Published scientific research studies, for example, present material in order of the steps ordained by the scientific method (observations, hypothesis, design of experiment to test predictions of hypothesis, results, conclusions)—and gain validity thereby, even though it is increasingly admitted in public that the actual process of inquiry is often a jumbled array of flights of inspiration, false starts, journeys along tangents, and so on. Similarly, decision making is supposed to be based solely on rational criteria, and little recognition is given to the possibility that decisions may be influenced by unconscious "scripts," (motivating factors of which a person is unaware) and intuition.

The Third Wave accords validity to intuitive and nonrational processes, seeing them as important contributors to inquiry and decision making. The unconscious mind, like the conscious mind, is increasingly viewed as a source of intentionality—what we believe will tend to come about—and growing emphasis is thus placed on the need to be certain that one's unconscious and conscious beliefs are in sync.

People in the Fourth Wave will tap into the full range of human cognitive and perceptual abilities, including some we may not yet be aware of. The centrality of intention (what we believe will occur) will be recognized as the means by which we create a future for all.

Moving from One Wave to the Next

Our metaphor of waves suggests a passive element to change that does not exist in reality. The transitions from the Second Wave to the Third Wave and then the Fourth Wave will involve many dislocations, often very painful but nonetheless with the highest reward. We turn now to a characterization of the major shifts corporations will undertake in moving from one wave to the next.

CORPORATE ROLE

The Second Wave
Maximize profits

The Third Wave
Create value

The Fourth Wave
Act as global steward

THREE

A New Role for Business: Global Stewardship

THE UNITED STATES and the world as a whole are facing major crises. In this critical period, we endure political candidates whose electoral success is due to thirty-second sound bites and cleverly crafted television appearances—formats that ensure popularity contests rather than elections of transformative leaders who will give pressing local, national, and global problems the attention they need. We also find few who are widely recognized as transformative leaders in churches, schools, colleges, or social institutions.

Where might we look to fill this need for transformative leadership? The answer, suggested by many futurists and consultants, is both surprising and inspiring: businesspeople will become more prominent as global and transformative leaders in the future.

The Responsibility of Business

The business of business is not only business. In recent
decades, business has emerged as the dominant institution
in global culture (Hawken 1992). The other institutions of
society—political, educational, religious, social—have a
decreasing ability to offer effective leadership: their resources
limited, their following fragmented, their legitimacy increasingly questioned, politicians, academics, priests, and
proselytizers have neither the resources nor the flexibility
to mount an effective response to the manifold challenges
we are facing. Business, by default, must begin to assume
responsibility for the whole.

This responsibility has never been within the purview of
business. The growing demand for responsible leadership from
the business sector is, however, forcing a shift away from
conducting business purely for profit toward providing a wider
range of stewardship (Moskowitz 1992; Cox 1991; Forest 1991;
Norton 1991). Ryuzaburo Kaku (1992, 5), chairman of Canon,
Inc., has acknowledged this imperative: "In the world of the
twenty-first century, the private sector will have both the possibility and the responsibility of overtaking the public sector as
the basic provider of wealth and stability around the globe."

An early indicator of this shift is the increasing attention
given to protecting our physical environment and ecosystems.
Corporations are being asked to do more than just clean up
their own mess—and increasing numbers are responding.
Recent group initiatives include an alliance of twenty-five companies, including McDonald's, 3M, Bank of America, and Du
Pont, formed to develop and expand markets for recycled

products (Allen 1992), and the Business Council for Sustainable Development, an international body composed of fifty business leaders (Schmidheiny 1992).

This trend toward greater stewardship will continue and is likely to be in spite of the opposition and foot dragging of many current business leaders. Our opinion, quite simply, is that if business does not step up to fill this stewardship role, including providing responsible transformative leadership, the public, through their political representatives, will force business to do so.

As contemporary futurists, social and business analysts, and businesspersons such as Anita Roddick, John Carlzon, Ted Turner, and John Sculley ("Executive Transformation" 1991) see this challenge, business must begin to identify the needs of the planet and move to fill these needs. In doing so, business will take on a much wider range of activities and, more importantly, come to be redefined in the process.

The Demand for Change

How to get our corporations to change? Our first task is to realize that we can no longer afford to hide the truth or shrink from telling the truth about everything. Only when we have organizational climates of full honesty and openness will it be possible to move forward. Second, we must recognize the pressing need for corporate change, a need driven by the growing shift in consciousness we described in Chapter One. People increasingly seek integrity throughout all spheres of life; many corporations with serious internal dysfunctionality will not survive the next decade (Euler 1992).

The company of today must recognize and grapple with hard realities: many of our corporate actions are environmentally unsound. The structure of our governance systems causes unnecessary conflict. A split exists between our thinking and actions, such that we fail to "walk our talk," and much of our employees' energy goes into repression, hiding the truth, concealing problems, and refusing to face reality. People have neither the space nor the awareness of ways to get out of the box they find themselves in. Exacerbating this is the fact that in most corporations there is little tolerance for insubordination or public criticism.

This feeling of being boxed in is also exacerbated by the proclamation to managers, "If you can't do it, I'll find someone who can!" perhaps the most powerful whip that a higher level manager has to force compliance from a lower level manager. This statement is used often and generally with favorable results, since visibly losing one's position or authority is the ultimate disgrace for many, if not most, business executives. Implicit in it are the demands that change must be achieved instantaneously and that performance in the new state must be equal to or superior to the state one is leaving. This, of course, is impossible except in the rarest of circumstances. Therefore, for the "prudent" business executive, the safest option is to remain firmly planted in what is known (that is, the old way) and to implement actions that are felt to be the most controllable. In situations where this mode of operating is not sufficient (where demands are truly different from past expectations), the preferred course most often is to "fake it" or simply provide lip service and wait for the fad to pass.

And we wonder why executives don't "walk their talk." It is safer not to.

The game is changing. Business organizations are being challenged to recognize and accept a new role on the global scene. What is this role? Business being asked to do nothing less than realize its function as the shaper of the future of the planet and as the leader of global society in ways beyond the purely economic.

From the Second to the Third Wave

In *The Third Wave* Alvin Toffler (1980) offered a description of the Second Wave corporation that flourished in the post–World War II period. Centralized and hierarchical, it was focused on values like profit, efficiency, bigness, and growth. It was derived from the army model, even its language and goals reflecting this military origin: survival, self-preservation, beating the competition, winning. Success was measured by the bottom line, the generation of profits, and long-term time horizons were defined as five to ten years.

The range of corporate activities was narrowly confined to business and things economic and technological, and CEOs were accountable only to their stockholders. Corporate attitudes and policies reflected nationalistic concerns, and globalization was regarded as a process of economic investment in foreign countries. Business was viewed as a way to make a living.

Such a model was appropriate when society operated in a Second Wave mode. But this is no longer the case. Both society and its businesses are moving slowly into the Third Wave, and

Table 3. Dimensions of the corporate role

	Second Wave	Third Wave	Fourth Wave
Goals	Maximize profits	Create value	Serve as global steward
Motivation	Make money	Make money and help solve societal problems	Leave valuable legacy for the future
Values	Profit, growth, control	Creating value, trust, learning	Responsibility for the whole, service, personal fulfillment
Stakeholders	Owners of business, stockholders	Stockholders, employees, families, suppliers, customers, communities, government	Stockholders, employees, families, suppliers, customers, communities, government, ecosystems, Gaia
Outlook	Self-preservation; business as a way to make a living	Cooperation; business as a way for people to grow and serve	Unity; business as a means to actively promote economic and social justice
Domain	National and local; 5–10 years in future	International; share responsibility for the welfare of local, national, and global communities; decades in future	Global; share leadership in local, national, and global affairs; generations or centuries in future

as societal norms are being redefined, business is responding. Toffler saw the Third Wave company being "demassified," that is, broken into smaller units of greater variety, and coming to prize diversity and differentiation.

Besides being demassified, the contemporary corporation is being increasingly held responsible for producing solutions to societal problems (Fowler 1992). The public is more and more frequently looking to business to design new technologies, to institute new procedures, to share responsibility for the welfare of local, national, and global communities.

In sum, business is being pressured to become a more responsible and more multipurpose institution. Its original purpose of generating profits through the production and distribution of goods and services must continue for the company to survive, but in Third Wave society, business is also coming to be regarded as the producer of moral effects (Forest 1991), the creator of much more than a financial bottom line.

Perspectives are enlarging: time horizons are being expanded to decades; corporations are beginning to think in international terms and becoming responsive to the demand for a new international economic order; and globalization is being redefined to include addressing issues that cross national borders, for example, the problems of environmental destruction and pollution that were addressed at the Earth Summit held in Brazil in June 1992.

The transition between the Second and Third Waves entails the corporation coming to see itself as a creator of value. Its philosophy of doing business undergoes a profound shift as it focuses more on serving the needs of its various stakeholders (now defined as all parties who have a relationship to the firm, not just its owners) than on production per se. This is done in the belief that if the corporation serves the customer, employee, and community, then the customer, employee, and community will serve it (Bennett 1991; Norton 1991). Strategic thinking is reoriented to anticipate future needs independent of the corporation, and business is increasingly regarded as a vehicle through which people can grow and serve others.

A host of new questions epitomizes the shift from Second to Third Waves: The old "Are we making money?" becomes "Are we creating value?" "Are we beating the competition?" shifts to "Do we understand the need?" "Are we gaining market share?" emerges as "Are we providing the right level and kind of service?" Asking such new questions and doing business in the Third Wave mode requires a basic shift of consciousness away from fear toward trust, away from the need for control toward giving up control, away from rigidity toward a learning culture.

Corporations will need to become "learning organizations" (O'Toole 1985; Naisbitt 1984; Senge 1990). The upcoming changes will be so great and will occur so fast that only those committed to continual and widespread learning—by managers as well as subordinates—will be able to survive. More than this, only a corporation committed to learning as a way of fostering worker empowerment (and hence providing an atmosphere conducive to creativity) will have the flexibility and innovative insights to flourish amid the tumultuous times ahead.

Our contemporary world, both in society and in business, is a confused scene. Our actions are primarily Second Wave. But our thinking, in the main, lies now in the Third Wave, and our corporate rhetoric reflects this new way of conceptualizing. At the same time, some business executives and analysts (see, for example, Sanger 1992a; AtKisson 1991b; "Executive Transformation" 1991; Cook 1991; Rothschild 1991) are envisioning a Fourth Wave beyond the phase that Toffler described as Third Wave.

The Fourth Wave

This Fourth Wave is expected to grow out of the trend toward widening the purposes of doing business. The Third Wave focus on serving the needs of stakeholders will continue, but the stakeholder base will be expanded to include entire countries, ecosystems, and, ultimately, Gaia. The operative question will become "How can we create value for all, including nonhuman 'customers' like natural systems?"

The Fourth Wave corporation will recognize its role as one of stewardship for the whole in addition to providing goods and services to a particular customer base. It will have shifted its self-image from that of a primarily manufacturing to a primarily serving organization (Harman 1982) and will act as a leader in addressing global issues, focusing on what is best for all. The model of servant leadership originated by Robert K. Greenleaf (see, for example, Kiechel 1992) will become the corporate ethos of the Fourth Wave.

The world has sufficient manufacturing capacity to provide for all the material needs of the planet. We do not need more manufacturing plants (although some may be profitably relocated); we need better distribution of what we already have the capability to produce. The modern corporation is well positioned to assist in meeting the needs of the people of the world for food, clothing, and decent living conditions. Our attitudes and self-definition are the only blocks to our assuming this task.

In this new self-image of stewardship, the multinational corporations will emerge as effective organizers of large numbers of people for the purpose of global service. Their powerful corporate infrastructures and resource pools greater than those of most nations will be reconceived as assets in the service of solving global problems. For example, multinationals might undertake a project to match the lack of manufacturing plants in a given region with excess capacity elsewhere, then arrange for the relocation of physical facilities and technology. In another situation, they might supply a range of different products, including those produced by other companies, as need determines. On the global level, they could work to create sustaining and sustainable infrastructures and practices in developing countries, and thus support the NIEO goal of achieving economic justice.

With the Fourth Wave level of consciousness that will manifest in the twenty-first century, business will define its role as one of steward, helping to ease the transition from poverty to prosperity. For those "customers" who are entire countries or global regions, business will apply its management skills and corporate resources to solving the complex array of problems they face.

The temporal horizon of the Fourth Wave corporation will be generations or even centuries, consistent with its role as global steward. Strategic planning will focus on leaving a valuable legacy for the future, and business will be viewed as a means to gain personal fulfillment and serve others.

Our vision may seem outlandish, given the current Second Wave activities and Third Wave thinking, but once we have moved as a culture into the Fourth Wave, such conceptualizations will not appear so bizarre. Eventually, we will come to envision the corporation's role as one of service, and its customers as anyone or anything with a need to be met.

Moving Forward

Lacking a tradition of assuming responsibility for the whole, how can business move to this new function and accept a leadership position in global responsibility and citizenship? First, we need to make the intellectual shift from wanting to beat the competition to wanting to serve the world. Then we have to set as our primary focus the identification of local needs—as the citizens of the world define these for themselves (this to avoid corporate imperialism in presuming to define needs for others).

Third, those corporations that are already operating globally can recognize and capitalize on the advantages of a global organization committed to stewardship: its transnational character, its diversity of personnel, its wealth of global interests and distribution channels. Its worldwide presence allows it to overcome the limitations of proximal identification—that is, the psychological tendency to empathize only with those persons or events close to home (Gaylin 1990). Our home is becoming the world.

Fourth, business needs to recognize at the most fundamental

level that it is, in fact, a composite of the individual people within and appended to its structure. These are the stake-holders. As individuals, they are grouped into categories like shareholders, customers, employees, employee families, communities, regulatory bodies, and many others. Still, regardless of the grouping, it is the individual where the substance of and ultimately the power of business resides. In the words of Keith Darcy, a former senior banking executive and now president of the Leadership Group Inc., "We, as individuals, have the power to shape corporations and their policies. These institutions, in turn, shape who we are and how we behave. Uniquely, therefore, we have the power of self-creation. What is driving organizational transformation toward the Third and Fourth Wave is personal transformation at the employee, customer, and shareholder level" (personal communication 1992).

Today's business leaders need to encourage individual efforts to understand and modify old "tapes," the internal programming that governs our thinking, our actions, and our perception of reality (Rothschild 1991; Goleman 1985). They need to embrace those people who are willing to stick their necks out, who offer harsh critiques as well as visions of a better way. We believe business leaders must become commit-ted to proactive responses, eager to learn from the insights and experiences of others.

Acting Locally

Besides capitalizing on its globalism and becoming acquainted with the way business is evolving, the contemporary corpora-tion can make the shift to a leadership role in the world by "thinking globally while acting locally" (Henderson 1981, 355).

In the realm of business, there is now a widespread perception that being competitive and surviving on the global scene requires active, on-site participation at the local level. Physical facilities have been moved from the United States to multiple foreign countries, fostering the loyalty of foreign nationals, who interpret our American corporations' physical presence as a sign of long-term commitment.

Acting locally also encompasses actions as a civic presence in those communities where a corporation has facilities. For example, in the United States some companies encourage recycling programs and fund educational programs in local schools; their employees serve on joint corporate/citizen committees that determine community needs and directions. Some businesses even examine the civic activities of their employees when considering compensation and eligibility for promotion.

A cursory reading of business magazines such as *Fortune* indicates that over the last few years many businesspersons have made a concerted effort to care about things beyond the immediate business of the corporation (see, for example, "Not Business As Usual" 1992; "The Battle for Control" 1992; Hawken 1992; Kelly 1992). For example, David Kearns of Xerox accepted a Bush administration position as Deputy Secretary of Education, and Ed Woolard of Du Pont has championed efforts on the environment. This trend is likely to continue, given current realities. Increasing numbers of people realize that only if the whole is healthy will our businesses be healthy. Taking responsible, proactive, aggressive action to serve the whole is good business.

Thinking Globally

Multinational corporations have, of course, been taking a global perspective for many years. But in the future, this will come to mean more than it has meant traditionally. Our global perspective will extend beyond those places where we have manufacturing plants and personnel to include a sense of responsibility for the whole planet. Thinking globally recognizes that the Earth is one.

Beyond the environmental reality of one Earth, current trends suggest the emergence of an interlinked economy, played out in a "borderless world" (Ohmae 1990), that focuses on the common interests of all people. There is talk of the evolution of a "third way" economic form, beyond both communism and capitalism, an evolution of democracy that would integrate the entrepreneurial spirit of capitalism with an enlightened concern for social responsibility (Mollner 1988). This is consistent with the growing recognition that people cannot be kept in poverty in perpetuity: the demands for economic justice by NIEO spokespersons, for example, cannot be ignored. Accepting the implications of the fact that "we are one," business leaders need to face the challenge of responding to the needs of Southern Hemisphere countries.

As the Third Wave moves through our society and business systems, we are likely to see this corporate sense of responsibility evolve into a goal or vision of the corporation that is far beyond how we currently conceive our business organizations and their proper realm of action.

CORPORATE WEALTH

The Second Wave
Tangible assets

The Third Wave
Tangible and intangible assets

The Fourth Wave
Mostly intangible assets,
emphasizing the quality of life

FOUR

Corporate Wealth Redefined

THE NEED TO REDEFINE corporate wealth is a consequence of the corporation's moving out of its current parochial and Second Wave view of itself and its role in the world into the larger Third and Fourth Wave roles we described in the previous chapter. As business assumes increasing responsibility for the whole, new definitions of wealth will be created, ownership will be reconfigured, assets will increase in variety, and new ways of measuring performance will be adopted.

New Definitions of Wealth

Wealth in the Second Wave is defined as physical assets and is evaluated in terms of the traditional balance sheet. The focus is short term, for example, increasing earnings 5 percent this quarter over last quarter's performance. Despite much talk about the value of creativity and innovation, little or no concrete support and encouragement is given to those workers who manifest these qualities. This discrepancy is due in large part to the fact that the biggest drivers of corporate business today are product quality and lowering costs (via "back to basics") (Land & Jarman 1992). When driven top-down, such concerns are antithetical to creativity. They tend to lock people into fear, which closes down their creative potential. Rooted in the conventional, Second Wave corporations provide little room or appreciation for the iconoclast and hence little opportunity to benefit from this potential asset.

Increasingly, corporations are engaging in activities beyond the immediate purview of business. Progressive Second Wave businesses care for the environment as a way to improve their public image and promote the desirability of their products. Greater attention and benefits are given to employees to make them happier, with the ultimate goal of boosting their productivity in order to produce better business performance. All these decisions about how to treat people, the environment, and customers are fundamentally financially and management driven. Only as we begin to shift from Second Wave into Third Wave does our perspective rise above self-serving motives.

The growing sense of responsibility for the greater good that will characterize Third Wave corporations will lead to an expanded definition of wealth. No longer will wealth be predicated solely on the basis of financial gain. Less tangible variables, such as the opportunity provided for personal growth of employees, creation of an environment of trust and caring, and service to those in need of assistance, will also be viewed as part of a corporation's wealth.

By the time of the Fourth Wave, business leaders will have

emerged as stewards of society, accepting responsibility for the whole. They will have taken on a much wider agenda for themselves, one that means measuring and evaluating performance in social as well as financial terms.

Fourth Wave corporate wealth will be seen as peace, service, personal fulfillment, planetary and personal health, justice, and sharing, in addition to financial rewards for stakeholders. Given the very different sense of values in Fourth Wave thinking, security will no longer be seen as lodged solely in the accumulation of money but rather in personal inner trust and the certainty of the cooperation and mutual aid of one's fellow beings.

Businesses in the Fourth Wave will operate in an economic system in dynamic equilibrium. Under such circumstances flow-through (the consumption of resources) is minimized, while the use of physical stock (manufacturing facilities, for example) is maximized (Daly 1977). People (and corporations) will consume less and make what they buy last much longer. Planned obsolescence will be replaced by planned longevity and recycling.

Fourth Wave corporations will also consider questions we would not think to apply to business today: "How is the corporation handling its global responsibility?" "What is the corporation doing to improve the health of the planet?"

Reconfiguring Ownership

For more than 150 years, capitalism has been the subject of critiques for its tendencies to exploit natural resources and human beings and for fostering the concentration of capital in

Table 4. Aspects of corporate wealth

	Second Wave	Third Wave	Fourth Wave
Definition of Wealth	Financial reward from tangible assets	Financial reward and improved quality of life	Quality of life and alignment with the natural order
Ownership	Stockholders	Direct and indirect worker ownership	Communitarian
Assets	Physical plant, inventory	Plant, inventory, intellectual capital, diversity	Ideas, information, creativity, vision
Performance Measures	Financial accounting	Financial accounting with increasing use of social accounting	Social and resource accounting

the hands of a few. Concentration of wealth certainly has been a trend of recent decades in the United States. In 1992, it was estimated that 1 percent of the U.S. population held 50 percent of all the privately held corporate stock (Kurtzman 1992; Nasar 1992).

Our belief is that this situation is not sustainable. Redistribution is inevitable out of concern for economic justice, a concern that is likely to grow as the shift in consciousness we described in Chapter One spreads.

There are hints of this concern in the growing (though still limited) realization among Americans that they are, in effect, the owners of corporate America. This is not yet direct ownership with the control that direct ownership generally implies, but indirect ownership through the widespread involvement of many workers in company or group pension plans. Individual workers are, in essence, the owners of our major corporations simply because the large pension systems—such as TIAA-CREF and the California State Employees Association—hold so much of the corporate stock of the nation (Lohr 1992). With a few well-tailored legislative acts, effective control of these pension plans and thereby effective control of our major corporations could be placed in the hands of American workers. Why might this be feasible? A simple response might be that this may be the only way the American people can get business leaders to pay attention to their needs and to provide the leadership needed for a sustainable future. This could be the basis for a redefinition of corporate ownership in the Third Wave.

Erasure of the distinction between corporate and social

activity in the Fourth Wave corporation will change the whole idea of ownership. Capitalism as we know it today will have disappeared and been replaced by more positive images of humankind and a more communitarian form of ownership (Mollner 1988; Kramer 1992). No longer will other people seem threatening, competing, violent, or potentially dangerous, making necessary the privatizing of property. We see tendencies or initial steps in this direction in current models like the Mondragon cooperative in Spain, where a pervasive spirit of community drives the form of economic organization, and also in many of the intentional communities in the United States that are organized around a particular set of values and have an economic structure (based on, for instance, organic farming or the healing arts) specifically designed to support the values.

Expansion of Assets

Pressures to succeed in a global marketplace are, as we noted earlier, influencing Second Wave corporations to regard creativity and innovation as keys to successful competition (Chemical Bank 1992a; Hammer 1990). Numerous articles, books, and monographs have argued America's need to become more entrepreneurial. Within the corporation, on the personal level, this is taking the form of workers trying to become more "intrapreneurial," that is, more creative and productive within the corporate mandate. At the same time, many analysts point out the demographics we are facing, which mean a serious labor shortage in the decades ahead.

The more prescient business leaders thus see the need to view people as the corporation's ultimate source of long-term health and competitiveness. Walter Wriston (1990, 64, 68), for example, stressed the need to focus on "intellectual capital" in a business environment where ideas are "currency," information and customers are money, and vision is valued. John Sculley (1987, 98) of Apple Computer anticipated Wriston when he stated that the major investment of his corporation is in its people. The idea behind this broadened appreciation of people is that employees bring certain economic value to the company; their knowledge, resourcefulness, and creativity translate directly into earnings. The investment of the corporation, in other words, is as much in men and women as it is in machines.

But contemporary trends threaten the effective use of an expanded view of, or role for, employees. Virtually all large and most mid-size corporations in the United States and to a lesser extent in Europe are "imploding," a process that has been underway since about 1985 (see Figure 1). Implosion is the process of repeatedly liquidating assets, business units, manu-facturing capability, technologies, research efforts, market development programs, and people to improve short-term earnings and cash performance. Once the process starts, it becomes increasingly difficult to stop because the liquidated assets are no longer available to generate profits, and thus more assets must be liquidated to meet the new short-term expecta-tions. Unfortunately, one day there are no more assets to convert and the corporation collapses. A good analogy from an individual perspective would be the person who sells or pawns his or her house, then car, then personal belongings until one day he or she has nothing left and no recourse except to file for personal bankruptcy.

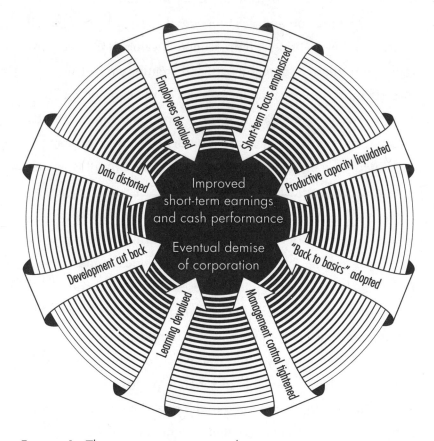

Figure 1. The corporation in implosion

Our observations suggest that, as we write, most large and mid-size U.S. corporations are in the third to the fifth cycle of implosion with little hope of recovery. While little can be done to stop the process once implosion is underway in a company, many business practitioners recognize what is happening and are working to try to cushion the blow as the system disintegrates.

Implosion is caused by the maintenance of antiquated structures and a myopic focus on short-term earnings performance. Highly centralized organizations face a greater risk because their systems are predicated on the idea of control.

Intensifying the speed and severity of implosion is the "back to basics" movement (Land & Jarman 1992). This backlash against change is rooted in fear, which limits an executive's perception of reality and leads him or her to repeat fruitless, nonproductive activities. Many managers in highly matrixed, hierarchical corporations have fallen into this trap as they tighten down their management structures, jump on the quality bandwagon as a new tool for control, and reinterpret the performance of businesses in terms intelligible to themselves but neither accurate nor truthful, for instance, by comparing prior years' financial performance for a profit center with current performance and forgetting to acknowledge a different mix of products.

Contrary to public proclamations, employees and learning are being devalued at an increasing pace as companies implode. In this mind-set of fear, "quality" comes to be redefined as "make no mistakes" or "avoid doing wrong." Such commitments, if maintained for long, lead to the demise of the business.

Rather than moving back to basics and tightening down, management in a time of implosion would do well to take a completely different tack, one that would move corporations into the Third Wave. For example, it could find ways to acknowledge its people for more than short-term profit making. It could acknowledge employees for supporting their team and other people's success. It could acknowledge them for deeds independent of financial value, for activities having long-term positive impact, for looking ahead, for thinking for the future, for being willing to take a risk and speak to outmoded practices that need to be scuttled and new ones that need to be tried.

A second way business leaders might respond creatively to the challenge of implosion is to commit to a genuine program to foster diversity, to bring a wider variety of styles, experiences, and opinions into the process of rehabilitating the business. Currently, many corporations are pursuing aggressive affirmative action policies designed to bring women and minorities into management ranks. At the same time they are purging some of their most creative and iconoclastic employees— essentially punishing people for being different. Honoring and seeking diversity should be an inclusive process. Corporations must recognize that working toward genuine diversity is incompatible with the maintenance of hierarchical, nondemocratic structures.

Finally, and most importantly, the imploding corporation should make every effort to help its people feel safe. The creation of a work environment that feels safe is a complex issue, but one of the first steps toward it is the articulation by the CEO of a few simple, clear criteria for performance: What are the norms in this corporation for making decisions? What can you as an employee do to look good? These are the questions workers want to know and need to know to begin to feel safe. These criteria should be few (two or three, five at most), simple, and clear. They should be developed and announced by the head of the corporation and then repeated often in both verbal and written communication so that people at all levels can have confidence that the CEO is serious and not setting them up for just another disappointment. Without such a clear, well-understood set of criteria, people live in the anxiety of not knowing what is really expected of them or not knowing if their work is aligned with the corporate mission.

New Ways of Measuring Performance

Over twenty years ago, Milton Friedman (1970) noted that business's responsibility was solely to its stockholders and financial performance was the only criterion of evaluation. Currently, the more progressive business analysts realize that the rules of finance, while necessary, are no longer sufficient (Chemical Bank 1992b), because they are inadequate as a means of determining the well-being of either individuals or society as a whole.

Corporate performance in our Second Wave mode is still seen in terms of finances, expressed in the financial reports created for stockholders. Activities such as environmentalism are treated as a cost of doing business or, for the more enlightened company, are done in the belief that such things will eventually have a positive impact on the bottom line.

The Second Wave corporation reports its nonfinancial

performance—for example, the corporation's positive actions on behalf of the environment and local community—in the form of stories and vignettes transmitted by word of mouth, press releases, videotapes, public TV programs, and other such means. All of this "story-telling" permits a qualitative assessment of the business, without, as yet, a translation into actual accounting procedures.

The early Third Wave corporation is likely to regard non-traditional, or social and resource, accounting procedures that describe and evaluate how value is being created for different stakeholder groups as much the same sort of hassle they currently represent to Second Wave business. Such procedures make things more complicated because there are more constituencies to serve and a wide range of data to collect—data that are often difficult to interpret and fit into quantifiable form.

The concept of the "living economy" suggested by advocates of the New International Economic Order (NIEO) and The Other Economic Summit (TOES) is a possible replacement for outmoded economic parameters (Ekins 1986b). In this vision, economic equity would be enhanced; capital ownership would be universalized; the "conserver economy" (Hueting 1986, 242), where stress is placed on conservation, recycling, and simple living, would be the norm; the informal economy would become visible; and locally based economic activity would be human scale. New forms of accounting such as social accounting and resource accounting would allow the evaluation of business activity.

Social Accounting

The concept of social accounting arose in the 1960s, one

manifestation of the questioning of conventions that character-ized that decade (Leipert 1986). It challenges the idea that GNP is an adequate indicator of social and economic health and has as its goals demonstrating the full costs of industrial activity and differentiating between defensive and beneficial expenditures.

Social accounting challenges the "market-centeredness" of current economic thinking and seeks to determine the social costs of production, that is, how much people really pay—in terms of dirty air, polluted water, congested roads, depleted soils, health threats, and so on—to support industrial production.

Concepts such as net national welfare, social and demo-graphic statistics, and the adjusted national product were developed as a means of operationalizing social accounting. Actually implemented in the 1970s by the Norwegian govern-ment, these new forms of monitoring business activity seek to calculate into the performance of business the social costs of various economic activities. A series of variables are factored in, such as the costs of environmental protection and cleanup, costs for R&D, costs of urbanization and industrialization (transportation of people and goods, police and fire protection), and costs of unhealthy lifestyles spawned by industrialism (smoking, substance abuse, industrial diseases and accidents).

Resource Accounting

Resource accounting, a new form of capital accounting at the macroeconomic level (Ekins 1986b), has been designed to ensure that our resource bases are not destroyed. It strives to describe such things as the state of the resource base, the depreciation of natural assets, the depreciation of manufactured

Table 5. Elements of the living economy

New Parameters	Social Accounting	Resource Accounting
Concern for economic equity	Measures social costs of doing business, for example, environmental cleanup, transportation of people and goods, police and fire protection, and industry-related injury and disease	Monitors state of resource base
Universalization of capital ownership		Tracks critical assets, including natural resources, manufacturing capability, infrastructure, air, and water
Stress on conservation rather than consumption		
Informal and visible economies integrated		Capitalizes natural resources
Human scale		Requires business to internalize cost of environmental protection
Value placed on ideas, information, creativity, vision		

assets (the infrastructure), the use of human resources, and the maintenance or deterioration of human health. It also capitalizes natural resources, no longer treating them as the "commons" to be trashed (see Chapter Seven). To prevent this trashing, advocates of resource accounting suggest the internalizing of what are now "externalities" of production, so that the costs of cleaning up polluted air or water or of disrupting natural ecosystems would be borne by the company that creates the problem.

Third Wave business begins to share responsibility with its employees, the community, and other constituencies. It does so while still retaining the self-serving attitude characteristic of the Second Wave: its good works are done principally out of self-interest. This, however, will be the time when the new parameters represented by the living economy and social and resource accounting are incorporated into business thinking and procedures. The Third Wave will be a bridging time, a time when corporate conduct and record keeping will bridge the gap between the Second Wave model of straight financial accounting methods in use today and the markedly different ideas of wealth and accounting expected for businesses in the Fourth Wave.

In the Fourth Wave, social accounting will become the principal form of performance measurement used by corporations for the simple reason that the distinction between corporate activity and social activity will fall away: "corporate" will be "social" when the ownership and purview of the corporation have expanded beyond the narrow realm of stockholders and manufacturing. The value created by the activity of corporations will take many more forms than dollars or other currencies because the corporation will be recognized as having an impact extending beyond its tangible business-related interactions.

The democratizing of wealth will be matched by democratizing tendencies in the political and corporate realms. Seeing the corporation in this new way has significant implications for its internal structure and management.

CORPORATE STRUCTURE

The Second Wave
Hierarchy, matrix, business unit

The Third Wave
Team-value

The Fourth Wave
Community

FIVE

Evolving Forms of Corporate Structure

FROM A SECOND WAVE business perspective, no significant change can be understood unless one looks at the structure of how business is conducted. Organizational structure supplies the building blocks of business activity; it fixes the mind-set from which change is evaluated. In the Third and Fourth Waves, by contrast, organizational structure will be a consequence of business activity. To show how this transformation will come about, we first look at contemporary Second Wave models of organizational structure.

The Second Wave: Hierarchical Models

Second Wave companies, especially the large and very large corporations, are committed to hierarchical models of organizational structure.

Traditional Hierarchy

The traditional hierarchy, with its centralized, top-down control and staff organized to serve the boss, was based on the presumption that managers know more than their subordinates. The two classes above the support staff, managers and professionals, were considered to possess fundamentally different types and amounts of knowledge than those below them in the hierarchy; and managers were to be the decisionmakers. This line of thinking, which served us well in earlier times, is no longer appropriate. Most professionals now know far more about the particulars of their products, market performance, and customers than the manager could ever hope to know. The shift in information technology and knowledge is pushing the corporation toward a fundamental change in the role of management.

Matrix

In matrix organizations, functional areas are linked together by staff who work together in support of a common endeavor. But like the military-based traditional hierarchy, the matrix model is predicated on centralized control.

Synergy is one of the driving forces of the matrix structure: the organization pulls together teams with the information, technologies, tools, and business and communications skills to be effective. While this is good for fostering creativity, it also fosters divisiveness and imbalance between the different reporting lines within the corporation because team members— from technical, field sales, production, research, purchasing— report to many different bosses. This inevitably creates a situation of divided loyalty: to the team or to one's boss.

When a corporation experiences the drawbacks of the matrix model, its response is often to strengthen the commitment to functional excellence, which further shifts the focus from team performance to the functional areas. This produces a double agenda—one for the team, another for the function—with different bosses clamoring for the employees' best efforts. The resulting conflicts do not help performance in the long run. Instead, situations in which good, caring people are forced into conflicts and unproductive binds are created. Often, in trying to contribute, people generate results that are counterproductive. Not surprisingly, morale is generally very low, even for loyal veterans with many years' service with the company.

Levels of trust among employees are also low, fueling poor work performance, a lack of caring, and the widespread question, "Is this my job?" People, too often, are working out of fear of being fired or hurt, sharing an unconscious perception that the boss holds an axe over their heads. In such an atmosphere, the job might get done, but without passion or real commitment to excellence.

Other problems are associated with the matrixed corporation. Matrices produce the irony of simultaneous data overload and insufficient data. We hear managers complain about all the information that crosses their desks even as they bewail the lack of essential facts and figures—material that is needed because in the Second Wave managers are viewed as the source of decisions and control. The corporate response to this logjam of data and control is often to remove management layers in recognition of the fact that the spread of the personal computer facilitates communication and thus allows more ready concentration of the information needed for decision making. The managers remaining, now faced with a broader span of control, often come to feel crushed under the new load.

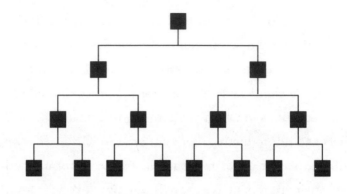

Traditional hierarchy

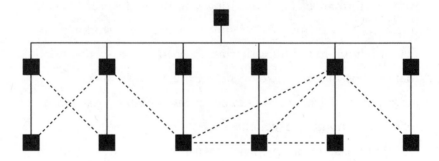

Simple matrix

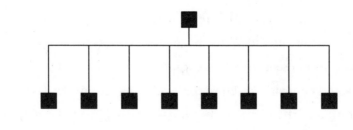

Business unit

Figure 2. Hierarchical models of corporate structure

In the flattened matrix organization, the manager is expected to play the role of coach while still holding the axe overhead in his role as evaluator. Consequently, the manager works in the limbo of a highly ambivalent, ultimately less effective position. Aware of this loss of effectiveness, many managers revert to the comfort of the familiar in a "back to basics" approach, tightening down wherever the system is perceived as "loose."

At the same time, the exponential rate of change in the world is pushing the manager to reconsider the assumption that merely by virtue of rank his or her knowledge is adequate to address the challenges facing the corporation. The traditional rhetoric makes many managers reluctant to admit they do not know. It also makes it hard for managers to read books, to ask questions, or to take training courses to learn to be better coaches, thus presenting a major barrier to growth and change.

The matrix organization lacks flexibility, putting it at a distinct competitive disadvantage. A matrix organization coming up against other corporations operating in newer, more flexible modes will lose almost every time, simply because it cannot respond to market changes as quickly or efficiently as other companies can.

In the 1970s, switching to the matrix form was a progressive strategy. It was efficient and more cost effective, it provided competitive advantage, and it fit with the technological realities of the day, when information was still the prerogative of the manager. This is no longer true today, and astute business analysts acknowledge that the matrix form is now as damaging to corporate performance as the old hierarchical structure was twenty years ago.

Table 6. Features of corporate structure

	Second Wave	Third Wave	Fourth Wave
Structure	Hierarchy, matrix, business unit	Team-value	Community
Locus of Control and Authority	Centralized, top-down	Democratic, participatory	Consensual decision making; everyone a leader, everyone a follower
Role of Management	Decisionmaker; serves higher levels of management and owners	Coach, servant, facilitator, advocate	Nonexistent
Atmosphere	Fear, lack of trust, low morale, resistance to change and learning	Truth, open and direct communication, collaboration; learning a high priority	Freedom of self-expression for all, openness and acceptance, equality, flexibility, lifelong learning

Business Unit

The business unit model, implemented when a corporation creates autonomous business groups, is a progressive Second Wave approach to organizational structure that eliminates many of the problems found in the matrix format. There is no conflict between teams and functional units; managers are spared the agony of conflicting priorities, and workers are spared the bind of dual loyalty. Being autonomous, the business unit has only one task—to recognize and satisfy the market need. As a result, its members are able to determine changes in market direction more quickly and make decisions more easily. Greater flexibility is inherent in its system.

However, the business unit structure has a serious flaw: its valuing of people and of other critical elements of the organization, as well as its direction, is highly dependent on the degree of enlightenment of its leader. There are few checks and balances other than employee willingness to speak out and customer willingness to buy.

Organizations still operating in the matrix format are generally reluctant to admit the superiority of the business unit model in flexibility and response time because if they did, they would feel pressured to change, and the changes required are not appealing: much of the old hierarchical structure and managerial power must be sacrificed in shifting to a business unit structure. Yet change grows more essential as time passes. Some leading business consultants and analysts are now wondering privately if highly matrixed corporate organizations will be able to survive the next decade. IBM's announcement in 1991 of plans to split into autonomous business groups is, we believe, a harbinger of what is to come.

The Third Wave: The Team-Value Model

Even though the business unit model is a step forward from the matrix format, it still does not fully tap the knowledge and innovative power of employees. As we look forward to the Third Wave, with its increased emphasis on satisfying the needs of all stakeholders and more democratic ethos, the team-value model becomes attractive.

Organizational structure according to this model will, as its name implies, be composed of teams that are organized around values. No longer will the organizational entity creating value for a corporation's market be formed in advance of the decisions on what value to create. The team-value corporation first identifies a need it wishes to satisfy, decides on the means to satisfy that need (value creation), and then forms a team to do it.

Teams contain within them the skills and experience necessary to accomplish one or more business projects. As the skills and experiences necessary for a particular project vary over time, membership in the team fluctuates, with employees moving between different teams. Movement is guided primarily through networking and self-selection: "Where is the need?" "Where can I best contribute?" "Where can I make the most difference?" "Where can I grow?"

There is a concern with nurturng people. Acutely aware of its responsibility for the health of every member of the business, the team-value corporation strives to foster each individual's learning, growth, and greater awareness.

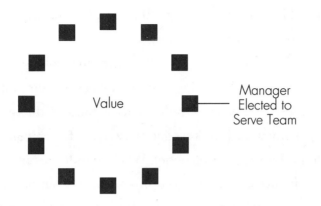

Figure 3. Team-value model

The team-value organization operates in an atmosphere of truth. Unlike the Second Wave corporation, where deception and unconscious deceit are omnipresent, the corporation organized in the team-value mode functions on the basis of openness and honesty. Its people are able to speak the truth without fear of reprisal. Further, they are in touch with themselves to the extent that they can distinguish what is real and what is projection (the unconscious "scripts" or schemas that appear when people live out of touch with themselves [Goleman 1985]). Communication in the team-value organization is open and direct; people know where they stand with each other.

As a consequence, there is a great deal of trust and collaboration. People work together cooperatively rather than competitively, with a sense of shared purpose: to make a difference in the world. Feelings of safety are achieved in this structure through bonding between team members, through their clarity of purpose, and through the absence of conflict in

agendas. The team's agenda and the agenda of the larger organization around it are in harmony.

In such an atmosphere of trust, cooperation, collaboration,
and safety, it is not surprising that employees feel empowered
and manifest high levels of both creativity and productivity.
Because empowered workers get more done, fewer workers are
needed in the team-value model. Where employees in Second
Wave structures are motivated primarily to stay out of trouble,
in the Third Wave they work free of that fear and so can focus
on getting tasks accomplished.

The range of responsibilities and obligations of the team-
value structure reveals its Third Wave nature as well as its sharp
differences from the authoritarian mind-set of Second Wave
hierarchies. Democratic processes are a key theme in team-
value organizations. All members of the team are responsible
for participating in setting the direction of the business.
Decision making is the responsibility of those positioned at the
interface with customers, suppliers, or other stakeholder
groups. Team dialogues produce the decisions, ranging from
how to allocate resources to member compensation and performance feedback. All members are regarded as prospective
leaders, with the position of leadership rotating as need
dictates. For example, a situation calling for guidance by the
team member with technical skill would make him or her the
leader at that time.

Where are the managers in this structure? The team-value
organization in general has fewer levels of managers than the
Second Wave matrix and business unit models. The span of
control may be broadened to cover as many as fifty employees

and is maintained through the active participation of employees. The manager's role as a member of the team is to coach and serve the other team members and to play the role of advocate for the team; for instance, in those times when the team tries to "sell" a proposal for some capital expenditure. The manager also helps to facilitate the interchange of team members as people move between teams on different projects. Quite unlike the Second Wave system, the choice of managers is made by the teams themselves, rather than by management higher up the corporate ladder.

The team-value model incorporates levels of management to oversee the operation of the whole and to maintain a longer term perspective on where the corporation needs to move and position itself. Strategic planning and financial and other specialized functions remain a part of Third Wave corporate activity, but these are regarded as simple functions supportive of the main work of the corporation, not as complex endeavors driving performance.

Lacking multiple layers for control and lodging the essential decision making with the team members, the team-value organization reflects the democratic ethos of contemporary culture as well as the demassifying tendency Toffler (1980) identified as a feature of Third Wave corporate change. Besides providing a business model on a more human scale than the current enormous corporation, the team-value organization has the advantage of being able to handle the issue of diversity better than Second Wave models.

As units operating on a local basis, teams are able to be aware of and sensitive to the issues of cultural diversity and ethnic

Table 7. Comparison of models of corporate structure

	Matrix	Business Unit	Team-Value	Community
Role	Satisfy needs of management, make profit	Satisfy market needs, make profit	Satisfy market and social needs	Satisfy needs of all stakeholders, including Gaia
Motive	Survival	Survival	Creation of value	Service
Goal	Beat competition	Beat competition	Everyone wins	Sustainability
Metaphor	War	War	Business as a competitive game	Poem or painting: the art of creation
View of Customer	Consumer	Consumer	Anyone with a need to fill	Anyone or anything with a need to fill
Focus	Management	Business	Value	Community

difference, of which the Second Wave corporation is almost totally oblivious. Given the collaborative bonding within the teams, the support and guidance necessary to incorporate diversity into the workplace are at hand, so women and minorities find the team-based organization a more congenial atmosphere.

Like the business unit model, the team-value concept has the advantage of being able to respond faster to market needs and serves to shift the power to the customer, a main focus of the business. The team-value model also enhances productivity—it gets management off the backs of the employees (there is no boss), freeing them from fear and allowing them to tap into their creativity, thus promoting innovation and change.

All these advantages notwithstanding, there are problems associated with moving to this Third Wave model. Some of these are institutional and psychological, such as resistance from middle managers, who have a deep personal investment in the familiar Second Wave hierarchical structures. Current championing of the matrix organization around the value of functional excellence appears from the perspective of the Third Wave to be an attempt to preserve managerial positions of power even though this structure clearly leads the organization toward failure.

Another institutional and psychological problem is the investment in centralized systems. Many people feel a loyalty to these expensive systems and fear the prospect of looking foolish if their system were determined to be outdated or inappropriate; hence they are reluctant to promote change.

At the bottom end of the corporate hierarchy, employees hesitate to champion a change because of their preoccupation with trying to look good. With the criteria of performance unclear, people are now spending considerable energy trying to guess what is necessary for them to do to look good. Conflicting signals generate confusion and anxiety. As a result, few workers have either the time or energy to contemplate change or more appropriate models of governance.

A fourth problem area is a tricky issue in human relations. Currently, many corporate employees regard lateral shifts as a form of punishment. We noted that the team-value concept is rooted in shifting team membership, which changes as project needs shift. People rotate in and out of teams regularly. Given the assumption that rotation equals punishment, the team-value concept is unattractive to many workers. Making it work in the Third Wave company will require a change in this perception, so that lateral shifts come to be regarded as something positive rather than negative. It is absolutely essential that movement be a self-selecting process.

Only the most progressive small and mid-size companies have made changes in their organizational structure and management that bring them into the Third Wave. No large corporation is operating in the Third Wave yet, although the team-value model seems to be the direction in which progressive businesses are evolving. Pioneering efforts with self-directed work teams are underway, for example, at Hughes Aircraft, XEL Communications, and Weyerhaeuser, to name just a few cases.

The Fourth Wave: The Community Organization Model

The Third Wave team-value organization will be the antecedent of another, even more progressive organizational structure that will distinguish Fourth Wave companies: the community organization.

The choice of "community" as a label for the new form derives from M. Scott Peck's (1987, 59) use of the term to refer to a "group of individuals who have learned how to communicate honestly with each other, whose relationships go deeper than their masks of composure, and who have developed some significant commitment to . . . make others' condition our own." Like a great number of contemporary social critics, Peck is aware of the dearth of community spirit and concern for the well-being of the collective, given our American penchant for rugged individualism. At the same time, he is also aware of the need for individuals to feel they belong and that they make a difference in the world. Hence, community becomes a way of doing business as well as living that supports the individual in the context of being with others.

The community model will incorporate many of the features of the team-value organization—its democratic, participatory nature, its shared vision, its focus on customer and community—and then go beyond them to focus on cocreation, equality, and maximal flexibility.

It will approach on the collective level what psychological and spiritual maturity, or individuation, looks like for the individual. The individuated corporation following a community model assumes the freedom of self-expression for

Figure 4. Community model of organizational structure

all its members (Stein 1990). People will feel safe. There will
be a complete absence of hierarchy, with no management levels
needed because the shift in the locus of authority will by then
be complete; people will shift roles from leader to follower as
needs dictate. External evaluators, regulators, coaches, and
intermediaries will be unnecessary.

With a deep sense of trust pervading the corporate ethos,
individuals will be honored as the unique beings they are
and also as part of the whole. Communication will be easier,
since the viewpoint of each individual will be honored,
thereby creating the space for individuals with different
views to "get on the same wavelength" and to discover
where they share similar values, standards, and expectations.
Decision making throughout the organization will be

consistent with its members' shared vision, principles, and values.

Issues that now provoke great anxiety, like performance reviews and determination of compensation, will either disappear completely in the community model or will be decided by group dialogue. Money will cease to be a motivator in the Fourth Wave consciousness, replaced by the quest for lifelong learning.

A democratic process, perhaps one built on developing group consensus, will be the way corporate directions are determined in the Fourth Wave company. In charting its path for the future, the group will take advantage of the full range of human abilities, including deep intuition.

CORPORATE COMMUNITY

The Second Wave
Employees, separated by
interpersonal barriers

The Third Wave
Employees and their families,
with interpersonal barriers
increasingly let down

The Fourth Wave
Everyone whose life is touched,
unified and fully open
to one another

SIX

The Corporation as Community

A HOST OF ISSUES—environmental, urban, ethnic, and feminist—is forcing contemporary culture to devalue traditional Western individualism in favor of more appreciation of people as members of groups (Bellah et al. 1985, 1991). The contemporary *geist* now recognizes the tremendous benefits— to both individuals and to the corporate bottom line—of a strong sense of community. The very word "community" falls freely from the lips of such varied figures as President Clinton (1992), Willard Gaylin, president of the Hastings Center (1990), and Paul Newman, the movie star (Anders 1990), each of whom has strongly advocated strengthening community in our towns, cities, businesses, schools, and civic life.

Community is manifested in two ways: as a group of people and as a "way of being" that unites group members. The first type of community is formed by bringing people together in place and time. The second is created when barriers between people are let down (Peck 1987). Under such conditions, people open themselves to one another and are freed from the feeling that they need to try to defend themselves in their communications. They become bonded, sensing they can rely on and trust each other, which produces effective team efforts. When people achieve this feeling of community, their subsequent achievements are nothing short of miraculous. Such community building will enable the transition from the Second to the Third and then to the Fourth Wave.

Building Community

Business corporations need to create both a context for and an ethos of community.

Context for Community

By strict definition, the people employed by a company form a community: an interacting assemblage of people linked by a common endeavor. Second Wave corporations, however, have tended to view community as something external to corporate life. For example, until recently, a company saw little or no relation between it and the families of its workers. Employees were expected to do their jobs, with their family being one of a variety of outside issues they were expected to handle as best they could. Now we see the corporation becoming aware of the need to integrate the family more closely into the operation of the business. Most of this concern is limited to talk, but increasing numbers of corporations have begun to take an active, participatory role by offering such options as flextime to their employees (Toffler 1990; Miller 1988).

The Third Wave corporation will recognize that it has an internal community, one that extends beyond employees to encompass their families as well. It will deal with employees in a multidimensional way, not simply as cogs in a wheel but as whole persons with emotional, psychological, spiritual, and physical needs; family demands; and personal interests and concerns as valid and as important as their job. Corporations will articulate a clear set of pro-family corporate values that serve as criteria for employee performance, and they will provide time and space that enable employees to meet their family obligations; for example, on-site day-care facilities, scholarships for employee children, and resources for elder care.

In the longer term future, when women make up a larger percentage of our workforce at both managerial and other levels, the close integration of corporate work and family life will be crucial to the success of the corporation (Noble 1992). With feminization of the workplace, corporate leaders will come to realize that prosperity depends on viewing employees in the totality of their humanness as physical, emotional, and spiritual beings. At this point, business will shift into a Fourth Wave perspective, taking a leadership position to ensure the overall health and well-being of its family members.

Employees will have reached a level of personal and professional integration such that their lives will have permeable boundaries: people will be able to be the same at work as they are at home. One will not have to have one personality and set of values for the office or shop floor and another personality and set of values for home. No longer will there be a need for false fronts or the studied reactions so necessary in the codependent corporation of the present. The environment—at home, at work, in the world at large—will be healthy and health supporting.

Table 8. Characteristics of the corporate community

	Second Wave	Third Wave	Fourth Wave
Composition	Employees	Employees and their families	Everyone whose life is touched
Ethos	People separated from one another by barriers	Growing bonds between people, barriers increasingly let down	People unified, fully open to and supportive of one another
Outlook	Deal with employees independent of the personal and familial context of their lives	Deal with employees in a multidimensional way	Strive for seamless boundaries between work and personal lives
Values	Traditional white male perspective; structural violence supported	Female and minority perspectives incorporated; structural violence discouraged; truth, communication, collaboration, learning, balance and moderation	All forms of diversity embraced; structural violence in all spheres of life eliminated; openness and acceptance, equality, lifelong learning
Support	Manifest concern for employee health and well-being via medical benefits	Actively encourage the wellness workplace with programs to address addiction and codependency, family assistance	Operate under a holistic paradigm recognizing the mind-body connection; ensure health and well-being of all

Community Ethos

Creating community is not an accidental process; it can happen only in the company that chooses to work at it. Businesses must consciously encourage the required levels of caring and trust and a willingness on the part of the participants to be vulnerable. Concomitantly, they need to create the foundation for community by following the pathway from hierarchical to team-value to community forms of organizational structure set forth in Chapter Five.

Often a group will experience community in a time of crisis. This time of bonding and collaborative effort tends to pass, however, when the crisis is resolved. To create and then maintain community requires ongoing effort by corporate leaders—and all members of their organizations—to achieve community renewal and sustainability (Gozdz 1993).

When community is created, everyone is a leader and everyone is a follower. The corporation becomes a collective lifelong learning organization (Gozdz 1993), open to all conceivable facets of knowing and doing.

Changing Values

Fundamental changes in the values that guide how corporations act toward their employees will provide the foundation for building community. Changes that will move corporations from the Second to the Fourth Wave, through the Third Wave, include the following:

Diversity Embraced

In some cases, business is supporting affirmative action in aggressive programs with the goal of providing role models in management for minorities and women. These corporations are currently making diligent efforts to provide these groups with the support and training necessary for their success. They recognize that demographic shifts in the U.S. population will produce a corporate workforce of great cultural and ethnic diversity in the twenty-first century (AtKisson 1991a).

The traditional criteria corporate managers have used to select new managers are becoming increasingly inappropriate, and new ones will have to be developed as the corporation moves into the Third Wave. No longer will it do to promote into management only those people who make the selector look good. This unconscious process simply will not work in the future corporation of greater employee diversity. Members of ethnic and racial groups resent this; women generally do not play these games. New strategies will be necessary and are likely to be a natural outgrowth of the Third Wave team-value organization. When a company is at the point where the workers choose their own leaders (a Third Wave concept), full inclusion of all races, sexes, and ethnic groups in the corporate community will be a natural process.

The achievement of a truly diverse workplace in racial, ethnic, and sexual terms will produce a profound shift in values and a richer, more diverse set of perspectives about the corporation's customers, goals, performance, and role in the wider society. As the shift in global consciousness we described in Chapter One moves us as a society out of the Second Wave into the Third Wave in deed as well as in thought, we will see a natural, easy falling away of the myriad unconscious assumptions that now plague our companies in their handling

of initiatives designed to create equal opportunities for
all people.

Truth and Openness Promoted

An environment of truth—a climate where, in the words of
one insightful Du Pont manager, "putting the dirt on the table"
is customary and accepted—is necessary for change, healing,
and growth, both in individuals and in business. Without an
environment where truth is valued, fear becomes pervasive,
differing from one situation to the next only in intensity.
Resistance to change correlates directly with the level of fear
in a given environment.

Moreover, without an environment of truth-telling, people
fall prey to ethical debasement. This leads to human rights
abuses, in which good people who speak out against evil are
destroyed, and other people, seeing their fate, turn away, retreat
into quietism, and turn a blind eye. Edmund Burke's prescrip-
tion for the triumph of evil is realized: "The only thing
necessary for the triumph of evil is for good men to do nothing"
(Bartlett 1968, 454).

People see the lies and abuses, the destruction of those
among them who dare to be bold, iconoclastic, creative. They
sense the lack of trust, the fear that is palpable in the corridors
and offices. They manifest the pathology of "group think"
(Goleman 1985) in meetings, where silence greets the manager's call for problems or differing viewpoints. Employees
in corporate America today live in fear of being seen as wrong,
of making a mistake, of being fired, busted, or neutralized.
Those with the temerity to speak truth to power usually
suffer for it, and the net result of all this is to leave the

Table 9. Examples of structural violence

Linguistic	Social	Economic

A host of phrases employing violent words or metaphors, for example:
  An idea just *struck* me
  I get the *thrust* of your argument
  I was *blown away* by....
  His look was very *forceful*
  We must mount a *war* on poverty
	Substance abuse	Glaring inequalities between compensation rates for workers and CEOs

	Spouse and child abuse	Glaring gaps between rich and poor
	Crime	Disparities between our living standards and those of Third World nations
	Recidivism	
Our dictionary definition of peace as a negative: the absence of war	Addictive relationships	Manufacturing processes that create disease and harm ecosystems

corporation stuck in the morass of the "party line," paralyzed by fear and deceit.

Structural Violence Ended

To be successful in creating a climate of truth and openness, corporations must put an end to structural violence. The concept of structural violence comes from Johan Galtung, a Norwegian economist and social scientist, who suggests that the very construction of Western reality is built on violence. This can be seen in the language we use, in the social structures we support, and in the economic structures we develop (Galtung 1969, 1971)—all of which foster inequality and division between people because they perpetuate economic and social systems that deny legitimate needs for adequate food, housing, work, clothing, and so on.

Structural violence is most commonly seen in the business arena in our management practices. Employees live in fear of being punished, of being intimidated by the boss and shown to be of questionable value to the company or to themselves. Even though blatant punishment is an infrequent occurrence, it does happen, and when it does, it sends a strong message to the remaining people in the organization to beware. For example, consider the situation of a mid-level executive with very high performance ratings over twenty-six years of service at a Fortune 50 firm who was reduced in job level to a frontline manager, then to a professional position, and finally forced out of the company simply because he disagreed with his boss in a staff meeting on how people were being treated. The people, the employees, did get the message: "Keep your mouth shut and don't make waves." Very few companies have a viable appeals procedure to handle abuse of this type, and only recently has progress been made on the issues of structural violence that derive from racism and sexism, such as sexual harassment. One company making genuine progress is Federal Express, whose appeals process is truly excellent.

Another form of structural violence is in manufacturing practices that result in ecocide, the death of plants and animals and the destruction of the life support systems of the Earth. Perhaps more than any other form of structural violence, ecocide by poor manufacturing processes is coming to be widely recognized, leading more and more people to feel that the way our corporations are doing business is not healthy.

Balance and Moderation Encouraged

The term "addiction" conjures up drug users and alcoholics. But addiction is coming to be more widely defined. Corporate consultants now speak of the corporation itself as an addict and as promoting insidious forms of addiction within its employees (Schaef & Fassel 1988).

How does the corporation do this? The stressors inherent in the tension-riddled matrix organization—arising, for example, from the conflict between business team and functional management's goals—that might drive an employee to drink come immediately to mind, but this is only one way the corpo-ration fosters addiction. Much more problematic is the overt encouragement of workaholism: the rewards to the loyal employee who pulled two weeks of eighteen-hour days to get a project in on time or the bonus paid to the team that never went home in a marathon work session that won a lucrative contract. These sorts of herculean efforts are commended in the Second Wave corporate value system. No recognition is given to the fact that these sorts of activities are reflections of addiction. That our puritanical American culture sees no fault in them makes them no less addictive, no less detrimental to our well-being as persons.

Another form of company addiction is the pervasiveness of codependency, or a denial of reality, at all levels of the corporation. Information is filtered, most often unconsciously, so that only partial truths are told. The parts that might seem offensive to the boss's ears are diplomatically left out. The reporting or discussion of bad news is avoided (the "elephant in the living room" is ignored) because people live in fear of hurting others or of being hurt themselves.

The result of such addictive and codependent behavior is that totally misleading information reaches the highest echelons of the corporation. (It will have been filtered repeatedly during its passage up the corporate ranks.) Corporate leaders, enlightened though they may be, are then unable to take proper actions, having received erroneous data. We are reminded of the vice president of human resources who reported to a gathering of employees that he knew of no situation where anyone was punished for speaking up. His belief was confirmed when no one objected. But only minutes later during a break, the vice president's remarks were the topic of conversation among a group of ten to fifteen managers, including some of his direct subordinates. There was the strong consensus that he was either totally blind or afraid to be on record with anything that his boss might object to. Clearly, everyone below him in the organization knew.

Table 10. Features of the Fourth Wave wellness workplace

Facilities	Health clubs
	Recreational centers
	Meditation rooms
Policies	Disease prevention
	Nonsmoking environment
	Incentives to quit smoking
	Drug abuse clinics
	Meditation classes
	Healthy food in on-site cafeterias
	Holistic approach
	Stress reduction seminars
	Mental health clinics
	Massage/bodywork
	Encouragement of use of psychotherapy and other techniques for integrating mind, body, and spirit
	Active support against substance abuse and workaholism

Across the country, in boardroom and bedroom,
contemporary Americans are beginning to face the reality of
this problem (Fassel 1990; Hawken 1992; Herman & Hillman
1992). Increasing numbers are aware of the lies and dishonesty
that are daily displayed in our midst. Many admit to succumb-
ing to such behavior themselves. Yet few are willing to speak
up, to point out this elephant standing in our corporate living
room. And since the pace of change is ever increasing, making
people more fearful and more reluctant to stick their necks out,
our problem is only worsening.

Employee Health and Well-Being Supported

An awareness of the value of the "wellness workplace"
(Naisbitt & Aburdene 1985) will move the Second Wave
company into sharing responsibility for all-around employee
well-being (Third Wave) and then into a leadership position
where the corporation includes the goal of employee well-
being among its other articulated goals and commits its time
and resources to that end (Fourth Wave).

What will a wellness workplace be like? In a wellness workplace, it will be recognized that the cheapest way to handle the
costs of medical care is by keeping the staff healthy. Preventive
medicine will be the order of the day. Health clubs, recreation
centers, and smoking cessation programs (coupled with rigorous
nonsmoking policies) will be widely available, provided by
the company. For their widely recognized benefits in stress
reduction, meditation rooms will be a common feature in every
company facility and workers' daily schedules will have
meditation breaks, similar to the currently ubiquitous coffee
break (Siegel 1985).

Besides being preventive, corporate health care in the future will be holistic. It is now widely recognized by medical researchers in the new field of psychoneuroimmunology that health is a phenomenon of both body and mind (Holusha 1992b; Weiss 1992; Yankelovich & Gurin 1989; Siegel 1985). The mind influences our emotions and hormonal balances, and these, in turn, affect our physical health: we make ourselves sick as much by how and what we think as by how and what we do. Therefore, the hitherto verboten area of health care— mental health care, in its various forms of psychotherapy and psychology—will come to be fully integrated into the corporate health care package. Where an employee in the contemporary corporation might hesitate to admit to seeing a therapist, in the corporation of the twenty-first century, doing so will be a mark of wisdom and enlightenment, a step on the road to indi-viduation, the stage of mature adult integration.

The Fourth Wave corporation will act to ensure that its com-munity is healthy and health supporting. It will also act to ensure the health of our environment.

ENVIRONMENTAL PERSPECTIVE

The Second Wave
Consumption

The Third Wave
Sustainability

The Fourth Wave
Preservation

SEVEN

Ecology and Economics: Toward a Common Cause

ENVIRONMENTALISM WILL SURELY remain one of the most common themes in the public media well into the twenty-first century, as our problems with pollution, resource exhaustion, conservation, and land use continue to worsen. Because environmentalism will increasingly command the attention of both consumers and lawmakers, the prudent businessperson will respond proactively to the environmental challenge.

Specific measures will of course depend on the nature and markets of specific businesses, but fundamental to them all, regardless of field or product, is the crucial step of changing attitudes. If environmentalism as a phenomenon is teaching us anything, it is that we can no longer operate from a Second Wave perspective where we regard environmental protection as a problem or ecology as antagonistic to economics. Rethinking some of the basic assumptions that lie behind the operation of business today can present many opportunities and can offer the progressive businessperson a significant competitive advantage. In this chapter, we demonstrate how retooling our thinking can turn environmentalism into a major new business benefit.

Ecology and Economics: Two Sides of the Same Coin

The coin here is *oikos*, our planet Earth, home of all life. Ecology studies the interrelationships of Earth and all its inhabitants; economics seeks to manage these interrelationships. As a science, ecology has been around for a little over a century and in that time has come up with some insights that could allow economists to manage the planet much better than they and their business followers have done so far.

Mismanagement has been due mainly to ignorance of the physical laws and operating principles of natural systems. These include principles such as the following:

The growth of natural systems is finite. No matter what the system, be it an individual human body or the global ecosystem, biogeochemical reality tells us that unlimited growth leads to disaster. In the individual, this is called cancer; in the global arena, it is called solid-waste problems and pollution (Murray 1974). Economic theories that regard limitless growth as desirable are as unrealistic as they are environmentally dangerous.

Everything must go somewhere (Commoner 1971). This principle explains why we have our current solid-waste disposal problem: the environment's capacities to absorb more have been exhausted. It is also the physical law underlying the necessity of recycling, which is also desirable as a way to conserve valuable natural resources and free us from dependence on dwindling reserves of materials such as oil.

Even more fundamental than changing our attitudes about recycling, however, is the need to reorient our thinking in business about consumption. Since World War II, to boost economic activity and maintain high levels of prosperity, Americans have been encouraged to consume (the more we consume, the more we produce, and the greater our growth in GNP), and entire industries have been reorganized to encourage mass consumption and planned obsolescence. Ecological considerations, in contrast, tell us that this is misguided thinking. "Consumeritis," as John Moelaert (1974), a noted Canadian environmentalist, called it, must come to be recognized for the potentially fatal disease it is.

Competition discourages diversity (Murray 1974). The basis for this is the competitive exclusion principle: when species (or businesses) rely on the same limiting resource—when, in other words, they are competing—they cannot coexist indefinitely; one of them will supplant the other over time. In contrast, economists would have us believe that competition encourages diversity and stability. This is not so. Later in the chapter we discuss how businesspeople might turn this law to their advantage.

The law of the retarding lead, or *The dominant species is slow to respond to change*. Ethnologists and ecologists (e.g., Keyes 1983) have noticed that change and creative adaptations to new conditions in the environment tend to be made by individuals who

Table 11. Business and the environment

	Second Wave	Third Wave	Fourth Wave
The Earth	A "gigantic toolshed"	A source of materials worthy of care and protection	A living presence (Gaia) and major corporate stakeholder
Economics and Ecology	Antagonistic	Connected	Integrated; operations are consistent with ecological laws
Resource Use	Consumption as a way to boost economic prosperity; self-preservation the highest priority	Values of unlimited consumption questioned; focus on sustainability, the sanctity of life, conservation	Focus on integration of life and fulfillment of purpose, recognition of all living systems, preservation
Environmental Protection	A problem; little or no stewardship for the commons accepted	A challenge; shared responsibility for stewardship of the commons	A way of life; no distinction between the commons and personal property
Opportunities in Environmentalism	Few recognized	Economic potential recognized; initial ventures undertaken	New industries developed (Sunrise Seven); old industries reconfigured to incorporate 4 Rs

are not dominant in the culture or ecosystem. In terms of business, this means that the new, small start-up entrepreneurial companies or the people working for large corporations who are allowed to be intrapreneurial are likely to be the source of the changes, inventions, and new techniques that permit long-term viability.

Nature knows best and *Everything is connected to everything else* (Commoner 1971). Ignorance of these natural laws by economists has led both to the "tragedy of the commons" and pollution.

More than twenty years ago, Garrett Hardin's famous article "The Tragedy of the Commons" (1968) pointed out that what we perceive as "common goods"—what is owned by none of us, or owned by all of us—tends to get trashed because no one takes the same care of it as they would of their own private property. Today, we rarely think of the commons, the old feature of common pasturelands in medieval villages and colonial New England towns. But they are still among us, in the form of our atmosphere, our waterways, our soil systems, our wildlife habitats, and our estuaries and wetlands, on which so much of our health and economic vitality depend.

We trash these commons today by violating the natural cycles under which these ecosystems operate. We see this in the phenomena of acid rain, the hole in the ozone layer, and land use policies that destroy wetlands. How are we to respond to this in environmentally appropriate and economically meaningful ways?

Suggestions include tactics such as capitalizing public goods (Sachs 1986); treating the public air supply and soil systems much the same way we treat such mineral resources as gold, silver, and oil; and internalizing some of the social costs of production.

Our belief is that ecology and economics are not fundamentally antagonists. They only are if we think they are, and there is very little to be gained by thinking in this way. By contrast, there is much to be gained by regarding environmentalism as a great opportunity, a new wrinkle in our culture holding many potential gifts for business.

Movement into the Third Wave

We are moving beyond the Second Wave emphasis on consumption, where nature exists to serve the human species; where we regard the Earth, as Clarence Glacken (quoted by Ehrenfeld 1978, 177) calls it, a "gigantic toolshed"; where no economic benefit is seen to derive from an ethic of sustainability and conservation. There is increasing acceptance of the need to conserve natural resources, to manage the Earth and its gifts to ensure that it remains a habitable environment for humankind.

Members of the business community have begun to actively embrace the concepts of environmental protection and sustainability. For example, leaders of some major U.S. corporations, including Monsanto, Du Pont, and 3M, have begun to take a proactive stance, framed in terms of moral issues or values, toward environmental protection (Cox & Power 1992). And the Business Council for Sustainable Development, an international body composed of fifty business leaders representing such corporations as ALCOA, Chevron, Nippon Steel, Royal

Dutch/Shell, and Volkswagen, recently issued a declaration that could serve as a manifesto for the Third Wave corporation. Some excerpts follow:

> As business leaders, we are committed to sustainable development, to meeting the needs of the present without compromising the welfare of future generations.
>
> This concept recognizes that economic growth and environmental protection are inextricably linked, and that the quality of present and future life rests on meeting basic human needs without destroying the environment on which all life depends.
>
> New forms of cooperation between government, business, and society are required to achieve this goal. . . .
>
> The prices of goods and services must increasingly recognize and reflect the environmental costs of their production, use, recycling, and disposal. . . .
>
> Progress toward sustainable development makes good business sense (Schmidheiny 1992, xi–xii).

Environmentalism in the Fourth Wave Future

The future will be a whole new ball game, in terms of our perspective on life, business, and the relationship between humans and nature. In the Fourth Wave, we will begin to see ourselves as one with nature, and view our relationship with the Earth as one of cocreation (Houston 1988; Simons 1992). For business in the Fourth Wave, the Earth will be seen as a major corporate stakeholder.

The nature of the transition from the Third Wave to the Fourth Wave is mirrored by the contrasts between conservationists and preservationists. From its very beginnings, environmentalism has been riven with different attitudes about nature and the proper relationship between humans and natural systems. This rift lingers today in the bifurcation between conservationists, or "shallow ecologists," and preservationists, or "deep ecologists" (Anderson 1987). Conservationists represent the mainstream of environmentalism today. They advocate the prudent use of natural resources for human benefit with due regard for the laws of ecology and for long-term sustainability. Their voices are heard in all the major environmental groups—the World Wildlife Fund, the National Wildlife Federation, Friends of the Earth, and the Sierra Club. The conservationists represent a Third Wave stance on the environment.

A much smaller number of advocates for the protection of nature take the preservationist view as deep ecologists (Devall & Sessions 1985). They hark back to the attitude of the founder of the Sierra Club, John Muir, in insisting that nature is best kept pristine, free from human interference. "In wilderness is the preservation of the species" is their motto. Deep ecologists speak from college campuses, a few extremist organizations, and as a splinter group within the Sierra Club. In their call for a fundamental spiritual reawakening on the part of people to the sacred quality of nature, the deep ecologists are anticipating the future consciousness shift that will move us as a culture into the Fourth Wave.

By the time of the Fourth Wave, the global consciousness is likely to be very different, with a correspondingly new set of attitudes. Earth will be seen as an entity in itself, Gaia, a living being with consciousness (Lovelock 1979). Humans will have come to realize the truth of Buckminster Fuller's (1981a) dictum, "We are not in control here," and thanks to this humility, we will no longer regard the Earth as a gigantic toolshed. As individuals and as businesspersons, we will have very different values: service and the satisfying of higher needs will take precedence over accumulating material possessions. We will work as much to serve the health of the planet and to fulfill our personal purpose as to make a living. Economic justice, recyclability, and sustainability will be key themes undergirding much of what we do and stand for, as persons and as business figures.

Opportunities for Business

Prescient businesspeople are already recognizing that the long-term nature of the environmental challenge will reorient the direction of global business away from industries that by their very nature heavily pollute or consume finite resources (Geiser 1991). Taking their place will be industries resting on the "4 Rs" of ecological wisdom: repair, recondition, reuse, and recycle (Elkington 1986).

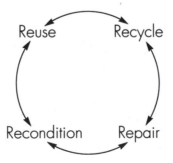

Figure 5. The 4 Rs of ecological wisdom

Industries based on these 4 Rs will flourish. So, for example, we see a future in the twenty-first century for businesses working in pollution control, recycling and resource substitution, energy efficiency, and ecologically tailored energy supply. These industries (along with information technology and biotechnology) have been termed the "Sunrise Seven" (Elkington 1986).

All these industries have clear wealth-creating potential: they have long-term viability; they conform to the natural laws of ecology; and they are appropriate to the more sustainable economic system that we will be moving into in the Third Wave.

Besides redirecting business into new realms, the environmental challenge also creates an opportunity to rethink how

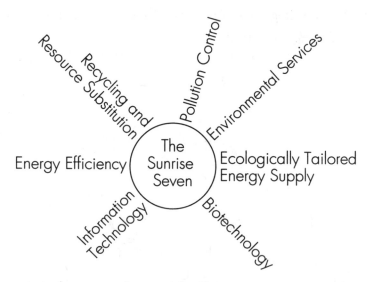

Figure 6. Industries with a golden future

business is operated, particularly around the issue of competition. Through the competitive exclusion principle, ecology tells us that competition winds up creating one successful species. Some twenty years ago, Marshall McLuhan (McLuhan & Powers 1989) suggested how businesspersons could use this fact to their advantage.

McLuhan noted that competition creates resemblance. By that he meant that when companies fall into competition over a market niche, they tend to grow more alike. The longer this process persists, the greater their competition, the less flexible they become, and the harder it becomes for them to gain market share. The way out lies in changing the rules of the game.

Savvy businesspeople can use the opportunities sited in environmentalism to do this. Du Pont's decision to opt out of the production of chlorofluorocarbons constitutes one such example. Not only did this move result in a public relations coup, but it also changed the circumstances under which Du Pont operates—R&D demands, different production methods and technologies, new resource uses, changes in costs and pricing—thus altering the competitive environment.

Environmentalism and technology use are inextricably linked. In the next chapter we look at what this means for the future of technology development.

TECHNOLOGY DEVELOPMENT

The Second Wave
In a vacuum

The Third Wave
In growing harmony
with sociocultural, political,
and environmental values

The Fourth Wave
In full accordance with
principles of appropriate
technology

EIGHT

Use of Appropriate Technology

THE RISE SINCE WORLD WAR II of a host of complex technologies has created both prosperity and pollution. While the prosperity has been welcomed, the resulting pollution has occasioned increasingly vocal criticisms of technology and of the science from which it springs. Contemporary critics of Second Wave perspectives of science and technology focus primarily on the limitations of scientism and the need for technologies appropriate to their time, place, culture, and environment.

In Chapter One we noted the trend toward the view that consciousness is primary, that immaterial things such as the mind have a reality comparable to material objects. This presents a challenge to the basic assumptions of scientism—which denies or disparages nonrational ways of knowing in its stress on the empirical testing of reality (Pascarella 1986)—and to the contemporary technologies that are based on it.

The current trend toward challenging scientism has led some people to questions about the dangers that may lie in cutting-edge technologies such as "algeny," Joshua Lederberg's term for the new science resulting from the combination of biology and robotics (Rifkin 1983, 17). Such questioning has further encouraged the appropriate technology movement. We believe that an ongoing assessment of the appropriateness of various technologies is an integral part of Third and Fourth Wave business practices.

Appropriate Technology

"Appropriate technology" has many meanings. In an environmental context, it is a form of technology that is benign, that meets the requirements of ecology. By using techniques and devices that are consonant with the laws of ecology, appropriate technologies do no harm to ecosystems and foster sustainability and environmental integrity (Elkington 1986). That we are beset with myriad forms of pollution these days is testimony to the fact that our technologies have not always been appropriate. Given the trend toward increasing environmental concern on the part of the American and world public, it is clear that inappropriate technologies that place life and our ecosystems at risk have a limited future.

More than just environmental considerations lie behind appropriate technologies. Cultural factors must also be considered. In determining whether an invention or new technique is suited to its culture, analysts examine the culture's population size, educational level, social systems, and pool of available labor, in addition to the resource base, market conditions, and infrastructure. Normative issues include examination of questions such as the following: Does this technology serve to enhance life? Is it driven by the values agreed on by society? Will it distort social priorities if adopted? Does it foster or destroy the social and economic equity between different groups in society and between different nations? Does it reinforce contemporary trends toward decentralism, devolution of power, and personal empowerment? Does it require elitist technocracies that erode the democratic process? Such questions are not purely theoretical; they have been argued forcefully by opponents of nuclear power technologies for nearly two decades (e.g., Lovins 1977).

As a value-laden enterprise, technological development is fraught with moral and philosophical aspects that advocates of appropriate technology refuse to let slip between the cracks. Americans generally have an aversion to recognizing the moral content of political discourse (Anderson 1987), but in the application of technology it is unavoidable. Our contemporary technologies, particularly biotechnologies like genetic engineering and algeny, are so powerful and so consequential for the long-term quality of our lives that public articulation of the moral limits of technology is now essential. Some advocates of appropriate technology now call for the institution of social, economic, and political impact statements for new technologies much like the currently required environmental impact statement.

We are being called as citizens and as corporations to new ways of thinking and acting in response to current technological trends. We must achieve greater clarity about what virtues and values we want our tools to serve. We have, for example, the choice of creating techniques that enhance environmental

Table 12. Features of appropriate technology

Environmental	Cultural	Political	Economic
Consistent with laws of nature	Technological sophistication matched to local culture and educational levels	Serves to enhance the quality of life	Creates job opportunities
Sensitive to the reality that nature is not fully known	Fits pool of available local labor	Consistent with societal values	Promotes better working conditions
	Congruent with indigenous resources and infrastructure	Fosters social and economic equity within and between nations	Allows a wide range of social and educational levels to participate in the economy
		Encourages shift of power to local and personal levels	Enlarges the range of human competencies
		Promotes democratic processes	Encourages creativity, initiative, resourcefulness, and personal growth

health, enlarge the range of human competencies, encourage personal initiative and creativity, and foster the development of our people. Equally, we can choose technologies that tend toward specialization, institutionalization, and centralization, in which people are little more than accessories.

The Fourth Wave deep ecology movement goes beyond the appropriate technology trend in calling us to an awareness of the inherent mystery in nature. More than being appropriate to its time and place, technology should be sensitive to the reality that nature is not fully known, perhaps not even fully knowable, and therefore we blunder into alteration of ecosystems very much at our peril. Deep ecologists plead for an attitude of reverence on the part of technologists, that in such awe and wonder may be born a concern for maintaining the delicate balances within natural systems that make life as we know it possible.

The challenges we face in our business efforts to develop new technologies and marketable products will only intensify. Several of these challenges are the inevitable concomitant of technological progress—in particular, our movement into the age of biotechnology, a time when biology and high technology become so melded that the line between living and nonliving matter gets blurred. Others are the result of the unique set of conditions we face in the contemporary world.

Challenges of Technology Development

The usual challenges of any attempt to develop new technology include the act of invention, efforts to develop the new device at a reasonable cost, and the task of making it accessible to the market. All successful industries have coped with these challenges, but today on top of all this has been added the requirement to carry out these steps in line with many political, social, and cultural agendas ranging from politicians' concerns about getting reelected to feminists' demands for gender-neutral engineering and design. No longer can technological progress be carried on in a vacuum (Boeing 1992; Pollack 1992; Steinfels 1992; Trefel 1992); corporations must include municipal, political, and administrative bodies in planning a recycling program, designing a new plant, or retrofitting a factory.

As technologies become more powerful and the pace of change ever more rapid, we face the challenge of creating more expeditious procedures to review the possible impacts a technology might have. Along with this goes the challenge of educating the public and business in the rudiments of technology assessment in order to maintain our democratic society. In our Second Wave companies little attention is given to questioning the impact of new technology except to the extent mandated by law. Broad-based education is essential to ensure that determination of our most pressing issues and values will not fall into the hands of "experts" whose objectives and values may be quite different from our own.

Another challenge for business and for the public at large is to discern between technology options, to become clear on our intentions of what we wish to create or have created for us, and then to act out of that intentionality. We are long past the time in our evolution when we can continue to act without awareness of just what it is we are doing. We must act intentionally. But most people in our society and in our businesses are asleep, living their lives in unconscious repetition of deeply ingrained habits (Tart 1987). Getting them to live intentionally is going to involve a commitment to lifelong learning, and that will most likely happen in the context of business, where most of us will work. This is another reason why, as we noted earlier, the business corporation is being hailed in contemporary business literature as a learning organization (Senge 1990). So it must be, if the challenge posed by technology is to be met successfully.

Some of the challenges corporations face relate to particular technologies in which they are involved. The field of agricultural chemistry, for example, is being increasingly challenged by environmentalists and advocates of appropriate technology to develop more benign methods supportive of soil ecosystems and in tune with natural cycles (Raver 1992).

The Sunrise Seven industries (see Chapter Seven) face the challenge of marrying ecological realities to technology. This is difficult and will grow more so, if only because of demographics: the number of students choosing to go into science and engineering is declining, and by the turn of the millennium our pool of available technological talent will be very small. In this milieu of scrambling for trained personnel, ecological awareness may have a low priority, but only technologies operating in compliance with the laws of ecology are viable in the long run, and only engineers with ecological training or sensitivity will be able to create such technologies (Stevenson 1992). It is quite likely that only the largest and most proactive corporations will have sufficient resources (experience and skill) to provide quality training in the ecological sciences. Few colleges and universities will have the necessary capability,

Table 13. Business's attitudes toward technology

	Second Wave	Third Wave	Fourth Wave
Development	In a vacuum	In growing harmony with sociocultural, political, and environmental values	In full accordance with the principles of appropriate technology
Creativity and Innovation	Dampened by organizational structure	Stimulated by a growing dependence on intuitive techniques and a team-value structure	Maximized by a full marriage of intuition and the rational mind
Choice of Options	Act without awareness from unconscious scripts	Growing awareness of the need for acting with intent	Primacy of the mind and the centrality of intention recognized
Assessment	No corporate forum	Corporations establish offices of technology assessment	Corporations assume a leadership role in technology assessment
Role of Ethics	Little or none	Ethicists employed to consider implications of technologies and corporate actions	Ethical concerns integrated with all aspects of corporate life

since only a few now require engineering students to study ecology (Fowler 1992).

As awareness of the importance of values and ethics, particularly in technology assessment, increases, the challenge looms to institutionalize the process of ethical decision making. Some companies are responding to this challenge by creating the position of corporate ethicist, an employee whose charge is to analyze the boundary conditions and strategic constraints on the corporation in the light of environmental, technological, political, societal, and economic factors.

A final challenge facing most American corporations in the context of technological activity is the need to reorient the process of strategic thinking. The typical strategic planning group in American corporations remains mired in the Second Wave model, with its focus on beating the competition. As we shift into the Third Wave, this must change toward a greater concern for creating value, which implies a concern for ecologically benign and sustainable, life-supporting technologies and corporate performance as much predicated on leaving a viable legacy for the future as it is on boosting annual earnings.

Technology in the Third Wave

Shifting into Third Wave team-value organization will give corporations the advantage of more open communication, greater trust, and more freedom to try new things without fear. This will lead to greater creativity in technological realms. In a business unit in one large corporation, in its brief history as an organization operating partially in the team-value mode, the number of new products commercialized in 1988 increased

500 percent over 1986, with no increase in dollars expended or in personnel. Besides stimulating creativity, the team-value organization structure fosters the likelihood of substantive assessments of new technologies and their possible impacts by eliminating the need to make the boss look good, with all the dampening of critical thinking that implies.

Third Wave businesses also will draw on intuitive techniques to help businesspersons perform more effectively and successfully. Within the last four years, we have seen a tremendous shift in attitudes about intuition, from a virtual absence of the concept in business in 1987 to the presence of more than a thousand consultants around the nation specializing in intuitive practices for the corporate environment (Pascarella 1986). Innovative courses and conferences on the use of intuition in business have been sponsored by such academic giants as Stanford University, MIT, and the International Management Development Institute in Lausanne, Switzerland, and by such business leaders as Du Pont, GE, Boeing, and Kodak.

In terms of helping the corporation meet the challenges of the biotechnological age, intuition will prove of inestimable benefit, keeping the corporation on the cutting edge and responsive to changing times. Members of a small cross-functional team of researchers from Du Pont are even now using intuition for guidance and problem solving in screening laboratory experiments, designing new products, and anticipating customer and market needs long before they turn up in the media as trends to watch (Pehrson 1992).

The marriage of intuition and the rational mind is proving to be an unbeatable combination for both scientists and salespeople. The company most skilled at developing and using the full range of human abilities will be the company best positioned for success.

Technology assessment is likely to be an integral feature of the Third Wave corporation, perhaps along the lines of the U.S. Congress's Office of Technology Assessment. A corporate office of technology assessment would have a five-fold role: to surface issues that relate to current or contemplated technologies; to carry out widespread discussion of these issues, educating the members of the corporation in the implications of developing and using the technology; to wrestle with various courses of action and determine what safeguards are needed; to lay out plans; and to organize execution of the plans. In the Third Wave corporation, all this will be done in a climate allowing open dialogue, the freedom to raise questions, and the opportunity to consider all sides of the issue of whether a certain product or technology should be pursued to marketable status.

The technologies of the Third Wave will continue the trends we see in technology today, such as exploitation of the Sunrise Seven, the mining of garbage for energy recovery, the pursuit of robotics and algeny, and computer chips capable of parallel processing. Such achievements will be made in the context of Third Wave values. Ensuring the health of future generations will be as important as creating material value, so that technologies will be pursued that are in line with the corporation's business plan (with its multi-decade time frame).

A Fourth Wave Perspective

Corporate technology in the Fourth Wave will be in full accordance with the principles of appropriate technology. Collaborative, cooperative, and imbued with a sense of internal authority, Fourth Wave people will no longer live in fear. They will see little need for competition, and their attitudes about information and the power it represents will be very different from ours today. Power in the Fourth Wave will lie within each person, so the transmission of information is likely to be free and may occur in forms much faster and more powerful than anything we know now.

Just as the communication technologies of 1790 seem rudimentary to us today, so our personal computers, phones, and fax machines will seem crude in the next century. We are also likely to make major advances in energy systems based on new mathematical systems, which will free us from polluting energy sources. It is quite likely that the use of fossil fuel and conventional nuclear technologies for the generation of electricity will be as limited as burning wood is today.

Algeny is also expected to play a major role in our future as biological and robotic technologies are married in the biotechnological age. Key factors in the evolution of algeny are the accelerating advances in computer speed and memory capacity and the breakthroughs in understanding the body's immune system (Rifkin 1983).

The science fiction stories of the past are now becoming reality, and this will increasingly be so as we move forward, our powers of creativity and ingenuity unleashed through the synergism of intuitive and rational mental processes. Only our imagination and our ethical commitment will limit the possibilities of what can be created.

We will have to deal with questions like the implications of these technology advances (Schwartz & Ogilvy 1979). Do we want these technologies in our lives? If a technology exists, how can we prevent it from being used or how can we ensure that it is used appropriately? Who decides who will receive the benefit of a technology and who will not? What will be the impact on our families, on our communities, on our world?

The potential for good and harm in the technologies of the future will make acting with intentionality and concern for ethics and values even more essential. This is critical: we are being challenged now as individuals to grow up in ethical maturity, to be prepared to handle the new responsibilities that the Third and Fourth Waves will press upon us (Schwartz & Ogilvy 1979; Pollack 1992). To help achieve this corporate action, to arouse in businesspeople an awareness of the need for change, to help set ethical safeguards in place, to see technology is used appropriately, and to assist the corporation in moving into a proactive leadership role will be the tasks of the corporate leaders in the biopolitical era.

CORPORATE LEADERSHIP ROLE

The Second Wave
Business leader

The Third Wave
Participant in dialogues on
societal and global welfare

The Fourth Wave
Global leader and biopolitician

NINE

Leadership in the Era of Biopolitics

THE ENVIRONMENTAL CRISIS, recent advances in biotechnology, and global democratization are propelling us into the biopolitical era. As we make the transition to this new era, business will play new leadership roles and assume new responsibilities. Here we focus on the qualities and responsibilities of our corporate leaders as they move out of the Second Wave to take on their global tasks in the biopolitical arena.

From Politics to Biopolitics

Biopolitics has been defined as the exercise of control over the future of life (Rifkin 1983, 237). As a type of politics, it is an amalgam of the usual elements of politics—power, connection, and uncertainty (Anderson 1987)—set in a wider context. In biopolitics, power is the ability to produce change in ecosystems as well as in corporate headquarters, city hall, or Washington. Connection refers to networks, or circles of personal contacts. In a biopolitical context, these go beyond

people to reflect the ecological law that "everything is connected to everything else," that humans are connected to other
living things and to living systems. Uncertainty is a feature of
all forms of politics, since humans are free beings and hence
unpredictable. As conditions in the world's ecosystems become
more stressed, uncertainty grows, making decision making more
difficult at the very time when it is becoming more urgent.

Biopolitics seeks to create and run a global social and
political order "commensurate to human power in nature"
(Anderson 1987, 9)—that is, on a level with our vast power to
have restorative or damaging effects on natural systems—
using sophisticated information technologies and democratic
structures. As the political trend of the future, biopolitics faces
squarely the host of environmental as well as evolutionary
realities we confront today. While we may be familiar with the
environmental challenges—dirty air, polluted water and soils,
the ozone hole—the corresponding evolutionary challenges are
not so widely recognized. These follow from our environmental
irresponsibility and include factors such as genetic mutations
that weaken the viability of species in the long term, species
extinctions that destroy the delicate balances on which ecosystem stability depends, and the need for humans (as the major
change agents of the environment) to consider multigener-
ational time frames in their actions.

Considering possible courses of action for their effects on
future generations is an ethical choice, a moral action. Biopolitics is deeply rooted in morality and closely linked with values.

Biopolitics is also based on a set of assumptions that sets it
apart from current forms of politics. For example, the scales

of space and time are very different (Anderson 1987): where we now see nations and gradual evolutionary change as features of politics, biopolitics encompasses the whole Earth, or the biosphere, and exponential rates of change. Likewise, the content shifts: conventional politics is a pastiche of legal, social, economic, and normative considerations; to all of these biopolitics will add environmental and evolutionary factors.

Where politics has always assumed the distinction between public and private, biopolitics will operate in a mode of action that blurs these, because private values will be seen as extremely consequential to public welfare (Anderson 1987). For example, debates about procreation will no longer be the private affair they are today, both overpopulation and individual rights having become grave concerns in the new biopolitical reality. With all these differences of scale, time frame, content, and mode of action, biopolitics will be a very different phenomenon from the political processes with which we are familiar.

In the biopolitical environment, no one will be able to claim he or she is apolitical. We all breathe the air; we all live in an ecosystem; therefore, we are all inextricably part of the political process (Anderson 1987). The very basis of biopolitics is the environment on which we all depend, and its fundamental issue is the challenge of coming to terms with the totality of the human condition. In this light, politics becomes a "process of moral growth" (Anderson 1987, 218), having as its goal maintenance of the Earth as a living system able to support human and other forms of life.

Seeing the Earth as a living system is a reflection of the planetary awareness that will be a characteristic of the

Table 14. Comparison of politics and biopolitics

	Politics	Biopolitics
Definition	Winning and holding control over a government or organization	Exercising influence over the future of life
Purview	Public life	Living systems
Participants	People	All living things
Use of Power	Control and guide change in the public or private realm	Create and operate a global social and political order situated in nature
Goal of Practitioner	Protect and secure advantage for constituency	Maintain Earth as a living system able to support human and other forms of life
Assumptions	Change is gradual and incremental, public and private sectors are distinct, people choose whether to participate	Change is rapid and discontinuous, public and private sectors merge, everyone is involved

consciousness of the Fourth Wave biopolitical era. Where environmentalism today is a growing concern, in the biopolitical era it will be pervasive throughout the culture.

Coupled with the increase in planetary awareness will be the awareness of personal power, leading to widespread citizen involvement in local issues. There will be greater concern for community, along with a "collapse of privatism" (Anderson 1987, 361) that may result in greater commonality of feeling among people. Such solidarity will be crucial to surviving the turmoil of the Second to Third Wave transition.

Wave Transitions

Getting from Second to Third Wave will not be without its hazards and hassles. Because change will be both endemic and large-scale, there is likely to be widespread social and personal suffering as lives and living systems are disrupted in fundamental ways. More than this, we are living at a time when many people are "waking up" (Tart 1987; Herman & Hillman 1992; Rothschild 1991) to a reality that is far different from that which they knew before. They are beginning to gain access to and be conscious of the enormous power of their unconscious mind, which is often a disorienting process.

Once we are in the Third Wave, there will be little respite. We have noted that the Third Wave is not the end point, so the changes shifting us from Second to Third Wave will continue and bring us into the Fourth Wave, in which business assumes a leadership position as a service-focused, multipurpose institution.

As a learning organization, the Third Wave corporation will

help its members make the shift into the Fourth Wave by providing the learning opportunities, collective support, and community resources they need to adapt and grow within themselves. As a democratic organization, the corporation will be equally helpful in supporting and serving its members, initially via the team-value format, then later, as the Fourth Wave takes over, in the community mode of organization.

The rise of biopolitics will affect business in some profound ways. This is obvious, since there is virtually nothing that business might do that will not have some implication for the environment, broadly defined. The result will be phenomena such as we mentioned earlier: the redefinition of corporate wealth and the development of new accounting systems, along with the blurring of the distinction between business and non-business and between the corporation's mandate as an economic organization and its mandate as a social unit. Such blurring will result in our dropping the notion that financial and social objectives are different; in the Fourth Wave biopolitical era, they are likely to be essentially the same thing.

With its products and manufacturing processes strongly affecting global ecosystems, with its personnel widely involved in monitoring these impacts and developing new products and methods to mitigate the adverse effects of manufacturing, the corporation will be a central player on the biopolitical scene and widely regarded by the general public as a producer of moral effects as well as of products (Forest 1991). As such, it will be incumbent on the corporation to institutionalize a concern for the preservation of the environment and the welfare of people and communities as a legacy to future generations.

Fourth Wave Leaders

In the shift from Third to Fourth Wave, the corporation will move from sharing responsibility with employees, community, and local citizens to taking a leadership position itself. The corporation's far-flung resources will come to be recognized as global assets and its leaders as global figures whose position, ex officio, thrusts them onto the world stage. As we noted in Chapter Three, business is being called to provide leadership in the world, and by the Fourth Wave this vision will have been realized. What will biopolitical leadership be like, when corporate CEOs help run things? How will these corporate heads come to power? And what will we expect them to do?

Personal Attributes

What sort of person will the Fourth Wave corporate CEO be? Prime among his or her qualities will be personal maturity. At a time when the corporation will have emerged from codependency and unconsciousness, its leaders will necessarily have done likewise. They will manifest a level of maturity or individuation that permits self-awareness of personal "scripts," or unconscious programming. No longer living in self-deception, these leaders will be capable of clear thinking and effective action. They will have worked on themselves in deep, internal ways, such that they will be able to control the innate human urge for omnipotence, which, given the prominent place of the business in the Fourth Wave, could present temptations for the less mature, with grave consequences.

Equally important, business leaders will be ethically sensitive. Supportive of the concept of cultural diversity, they will understand the full range of its impact on the company. In

147

Table 15. Characteristics of corporate leadership

Activity	Second Wave	Third Wave	Fourth Wave
	Politics	Aware of need for biopolitics	Biopolitics
Selection of Leaders	Appointment by corporate governing board	Top executives appointed by board; team leaders selected by team members	Through process of multiple, successive elections
Allegiance	Corporate and national	Moving beyond corporate and national boundaries to embrace the Earth and its peoples	Corporate and planetary
Responsibilities	Lead corporation	Lead corporation and contribute to public dialogues on societal and global welfare	Lead corporation, help create global political order, guide and influence public dialogue
Performance Review of Leaders	By governing board; bottom line is main criterion	By governing board; contributions beyond bottom line and outside corporate walls taken into account	By a global council representing all peoples; results of biopolitical activity a major criterion

the same way, corporate CEOs, male and female, will be in touch with both the feminine as well as the masculine within themselves, and out of this awareness, they will be supportive of the reorientation of values that the feminine represents.

In this as in other ways, the heads of corporations will not be able to ignore their role as moral leaders. Intentionality, the alignment of conscious choice with the energy to manifest that choice, will be their focus as well as part of their daily mode of living. And CEOs in the Fourth Wave will live intuitively, regarding their intuition as a tool as valuable as logic or reason.

Most important, Fourth Wave corporate leaders will be optimists, able to see the opportunities as well as the dangers in the mounting crises around them, able to view problems more as opportunities than as obstacles. With this positive frame of mind, they will be able to inspire and encourage those around them, a crucial ability, given the tumult we will be facing.

Selection Process

The quality of global leadership will be closely tied to the method of selecting corporate leaders. This will be so because of the culling and screening that will be part of the background of each corporate leader, whatever the size of the organization. Given the democratic ethos of the Fourth Wave corporation, in which community members choose their leaders, the CEO will attain his or her position through a process of multiple, successive elections during which leaders choose from among their own the person they deem most capable of serving their collective needs. Since the ultimate criterion will be the individual's ability to serve, tested repeatedly in interactions with his or her peers, this culling process will eliminate, or at

least, substantially reduce, the likelihood that the dysfunctional, the less effective, the ill-suited by reason of personality
or character will take charge of the major Fourth Wave corporations with their tens of thousands of people and enormous
resources and responsibilities.

Responsibilities

What will be their charge, as corporate heads at a time when
business has assumed its responsibility of providing leadership?
These men and women will operate essentially as biopoliticians. As such, they will have a global perspective and a
planetary allegiance (Gelb 1991). With this perspective, it will
be essential for corporate global leaders to have an accurate perception of the realities of the global condition—environmental,
cultural, and economic—in order to be able to recognize needs
and act appropriately on them.

Because environmental and technological issues will
interface so closely in the biopolitical era, business leaders will
have to be familiar with both the discipline of ecology and the
principles of technology assessment. One of their responsibilities as biopoliticians will be to address the moral, cultural, and
economic questions in the energetic discussions that will be
common in the Fourth Wave. Because of their dual allegiance—
to their corporations, as well as to the world—these leaders
will be well placed to foster close integration of the economic,
environmental, technological, and social considerations and circumstances of their society.

At a time when nationality will have become incidental,
these corporate global leaders will operate beyond nationalistic
frames of reference, interacting freely with other global leaders

to address problems relating to the environment, the allocation of natural and human resources, and technology assessment and application. In filling this responsibility, they will serve as global diplomats, dealing with nongovernment organizations, with global groups like the United Nations, and with regional and local governments. Their turf will be the borderless world of cosmopolitan post-capitalism. Their greatest challenge will be to participate with other such leaders in the creation of a global political order.

To do so will require all the personal development, interpersonal strength, ethical maturity, and wisdom their election as corporate CEOs will have suggested, for creating such a system will require our corporate leaders to act without taking flight into dominance (the "caricature of power") or into passivity ("the caricature of innocence") (Anderson 1987, 322), both of which have been notorious temptations to the men and women of our own day. Along with this herculean job will go the task of influencing public dialogue. It will fall to these leaders to suggest the issues people need to develop opinions about. In this way, they will be a major influence on the content of the debates about biopolitics.

As a biopolitician, the business leader of the Fourth Wave will recognize and accept the destiny of modern humankind described many years ago by Julian Huxley:

> It is as if man had been suddenly appointed managing director of the biggest business of all, the business of evolution. . . . He can't refuse the job. Whether he wants it or not, whether he is conscious of what he is doing or not, he is in point of fact determining the future direction of

Table 16. Profile of the Fourth Wave biopolitical leader

Personality	Abilities	Roles
Mature	Able to control urge for power and omnipotence	Global leader who is comfortable in the "borderless world"
Aware of own unconscious programming and inner character	Sees opportunities as well as dangers in crisis	Creator of a global political order
Feminine and masculine aspects of self are integrated	Clear thinking, effective in action	Influencer of public dialogue
Avoids domination and passivity	Lives intentionally and intuitively	
Positive frame of mind	Functions interdependently; inspires and encourages others to act	
	Able to address moral, cultural, and economic questions	
	Perceives realities of global conditions	
	Deals effectively with issues of ecology and technology assessment	

evolution on this earth. That is his inescapable destiny,
and the sooner he realizes it and starts believing in it, the
better for all concerned (Anderson 1987, frontispiece).

By the time of Fourth Wave corporate global leadership, we
will have realized the truth of Huxley's message and will look
to our business leaders to contribute the wisdom necessary for
directing Earth's evolution.

Obligated to the Earth, to their employees, to the citizens of
the globe, and to their fellow leaders, the CEOs of the Fourth
Wave will face an exacting form of performance review. Where
corporate boards of directors currently address this issue, in the
Fourth Wave the CEO will have to answer to the peoples of the
planet. This will possibly take the form of a global council of
leaders, perhaps chosen on a rotating basis, whose task it will
be to examine the activities of the various corporate leaders.
Such a global council will be an organization of enormous
power, workable and conceivable only because by the time
of the Fourth Wave, significant numbers of people will be so
highly evolved as to be immune to the blandishments of power
and public prominence and capable of guiding the destiny of
the world.

Living on the Slope of a Steep Learning Curve

As phenomena of the Fourth Wave, the circumstances of corporate leadership and global governance we have described may
seem hard to conceive. But contemporary trends support the
evolution of institutions and systems along these lines.
Between now and then, we face the challenge of living on the
slope of a steep learning curve (Anderson 1987), where change

is rapid and disorientation a constant threat. As learning organizations, corporations will help move society along this curve, promoting its adaptation and progress from the Second to the Third and then the Fourth Wave.

THE FOURTH WAVE CORPORATION

Exemplar for Other Institutions

Global Citizen Acting Locally

Advocate of the Living Economy

Committed to Serve

Community of Wellness

Model of Environmental Concern

Pioneer in Appropriate Technologies

Led by Biopoliticians

TEN

Business in the Twenty-First Century

CONSIDER THE FOLLOWING VISIONS of the new corporation:

As an exemplar for other institutions in society. See us becoming aware of the contemporary shift in consciousness and working to foster it, especially recognizing the value of intuition in business and using it extensively.

As a global citizen acting locally, while thinking globally. See business responding to the pleas for democratization of the international economic order and moving to implement it. Envision the corporation sharing responsibility with its constituencies in the Third Wave and taking responsibility for the Earth as a whole and working to heal it in the Fourth Wave.

As an advocate of the living economy, practicing social and resource accounting. See business reaffirming the value of its intellectual capital, thereby boosting creativity and discovering a host of new strengths within its ranks that constantly spin off new businesses. See us working toward new forms of ownership in the future and achieving global prominence for it.

As an organization committed to serve, aware of its identity as a producer of moral effects. See companies creating a safe environment for employees' growth and development and reaping manifold rewards for it, adopting the team-value organization in the Third Wave and profiting from it, growing into the community model in the Fourth Wave and being strengthened by it.

As a community of wellness, aware of the full range of its corporate stakeholders. See the company integrating the families of employees into its concern, and see it advancing the cause of affirmative action in its policies, thus achieving a richer diversity. Envision us tackling the challenges of codependency and addiction to attain greater levels of honesty and truth-telling and, ultimately, well-being.

As a model of environmental concern. See business taking seriously the principle of sustainability and working to create products and practices conforming to it. See many companies proactively involved in the Sunrise Seven industries, recognizing the Earth as their ultimate customer and developing ways to serve it.

As a pioneer in appropriate technologies, skilled in technology assessment. See corporations practicing the principle of intentionality and reorienting their strategic planning to incorporate it. See them establishing internal structures to reflect ethical concerns, creating a new definition of "long term" to consider needs for future generations.

As an organization led by biopoliticians who are fully aware of their responsibility to realize the destiny of modern men and women. See business celebrating change and exercising control over the future of life, grappling with environmental and evolutionary reality via new modes of action, and offering its leadership to the governance of the world, that the greater good may be served.

From Vision to Reality

Will these visions of the new corporation become reality? We believe so, not just because they represent a highly desirable future, but because they are the natural, albeit revolutionary, outcomes of a progression—already begun—from contemporary, largely Second Wave practices through a transitory Third Wave state to the Fourth Wave. We have articulated details of this progression in the preceding chapters; Table 18 is a summary.

Current business trends indicate that we will not experience the progression from one wave to the next as gradual. In recent years it has become common for businesses experiencing difficulties to sacrifice progressive practices that anticipate Third Wave circumstances—self-managed teams, for example— in favor of the practices they replaced. These actions represent a step backward but do not undo completely what came before

Table 17. Challenges we face in riding the waves of change

General	Business
Summoning the courage to speak truth to people in power	Creating work environments where employees feel safe
Recognizing the dishonesty in our lives	Fostering truth-telling on the job
Asking ourselves how we can move beyond passive honesty to active truth-telling	Articulating clear and consistent goals, as well as explicit criteria to guide employees' actions
Finding the courage to point out the "elephant in the living room"	Facing dysfunctionality within the corporation
Deciding to clear unwanted and unconscious programming from ourselves	Taking responsibility for healing the pathology in the company
Recognizing our personal investment in a particular view of the world	Accepting and valuing iconoclasts in business

because people have experienced a feeling of what can be. As increasing numbers of businesses adopt progressive practices, and increasing numbers of people experience the liberating effects thereof, the fits and starts will eventually add up to a critical mass. Change will then be unstoppable and rapid.

Many corporations remain wholly in the Second Wave. Others, however, have entered the Third Wave in some arenas. This is especially the case for issues relating to environmentalism and the creation of a community of wellness. Such a patchwork, or mosaic, pattern of change is likely to be evidenced increasingly over the next decade or so. As changes accumulate they too will reach a critical mass and push corporations fully into the next wave.

Riding the Waves of Change

The great change afoot within our businesses and in our society at large will not come without pain. We cannot stop the change, but we can take action to mitigate its distress by creating in our companies an environment where workers feel safe, by fostering truth-telling, and by articulating a clear set of goals with explicit criteria to guide action.

The situation in the American corporation today is reminiscent of Germany in World War II, when people confronted evil on a massive scale, looked away, and denied it. Once again, we are challenged to summon the moral courage to speak truth to power. We must recognize the fundamental dishonesty that pervades our lives and businesses when people are unable to see or to tell the truth.

This is not unique to corporate business; it is a pathological and pernicious pattern found in all the institutions of our society. It is pernicious because it is unconscious: we are not aware we are lying; indeed, we see ourselves as basically honest people, and we are. But we lie passively, by omission, by withholding aspects of reality from our bosses, by glossing over our imperfections before our colleagues. We live in the midst of a conspiracy of untruth, and, in such a milieu, we must ask ourselves how we can possibly move beyond being passively honest to being actively truthful.

The first step in this process on the personal level, perhaps the most difficult and certainly the most humbling, is to recognize that in some profound ways one's life is not working, that there are parts of oneself that are dysfunctional. The second step follows from this: the decision to work on oneself by taking responsibility for one's life and healing.

These steps are similar on the corporate level, for only when the leaders of our business organizations recognize the dysfunctionality can they take responsibility and begin the work of healing. In doing so, they face another task: to accept and value the iconoclasts in their midst who have the courage to point out the elephant in the living room when everyone else is deep in denial. These critics help to move the corporation closer to truth-telling, which is an essential part of the healing process.

Business success in the next millennium is clearly going to require moving into a new game—a different game that has already begun. The point of this book has been to call attention to some of the features of this new game. We hope that in doing so we have gotten you to think, to question, to see how we are all vested in a particular view of the world. We want to help business leaders understand just what it is that we are vested in, what other views and courses of action are possible, where we are going, and how we are relating to the world and to our corporate stakeholders.

Given correct information and time to wrestle with the issues, our society will make the right decisions; of this we are absolutely confident. But all of us must take care lest, by operating out of fear or an "I have the answer" attitude, we lock ourselves into repeating the mistakes of the past. These visions are offered to help us avoid this repetition and to equip us to create the enlightened corporations of the twenty-first century.

Table 18. Characteristics of Second, Third, and Fourth Wave corporations

		Second Wave	Third Wave	Fourth Wave
CORPORATE ROLE	Goals	Maximize profits	Create value	Serve as global steward
	Motivation	Make money	Make money and help solve societal problems	Leave valuable legacy for the future
	Values	Profit, growth, control	Creating value, trust, learning	Responsibility for the whole, service, personal fulfillment
	Stakeholders	Owners of business, stockholders	Stockholders, employees, families, suppliers, customers, communities, government	Stockholders, employees, families, suppliers, customers, communities, government, ecosystems, Gaia
	Outlook	Self-preservation; business as a way to make a living	Cooperation; business as a way for people to grow and serve	Unity; business as a means to actively promote economic and social justice
	Domain	National and local; 5–10 years in future	International; share responsibility for the welfare of local, national, and global communities; decades in future	Global; share leadership in local, national, and global affairs; generations or centuries in future

CORPORATE WEALTH			
Definition of Wealth	Financial reward from tangible assets	Financial reward and improved quality of life	Quality of life and alignment with the natural order
Ownership	Stockholders	Direct and indirect worker ownership	Communitarian
Assets	Physical plant, inventory	Plant, inventory, intellectual capital, diversity	Ideas, information, creativity, vision
Performance Measures	Financial accounting	Financial accounting with increasing use of social accounting	Social and resource accounting
CORPORATE STRUCTURE			
Structure	Hierarchy, matrix, business unit	Team-value	Community
Locus of Control and Authority	Centralized, top-down	Democratic, participatory	Consensual decision making; everyone a leader, everyone a follower
Role of Management	Decisionmaker; serves higher levels of management and owners	Coach, servant, facilitator, advocate	Nonexistent

continues

	Second Wave	Third Wave	Fourth Wave
Atmosphere	Fear, lack of trust, low morale, resistance to change and learning	Truth, open and direct communication, collaboration; learning a high priority	Freedom of self-expression for all, openness and acceptance, equality, flexibility, lifelong learning
CORPORATE COMMUNITY Composition	Employees	Employees and their families	Everyone whose life is touched
Ethos	People separated from one another by barriers	Growing bonds between people, barriers increasingly let down	People unified, fully open to and supportive of one another
Outlook	Deal with employees independent of the personal and familial context of their lives	Deal with employees in a multidimensional way	Strive for seamless boundaries between work and personal lives
Values	Traditional white male perspective; structural violence supported	Female and minority perspectives incorporated; structural violence discouraged; truth, communication, collaboration, learning, balance and moderation	All forms of diversity embraced; structural violence in all spheres of life eliminated; openness and acceptance, equality, lifelong learning

Support	Manifest concern for employee health and well-being via medical benefits	Actively encourage the wellness workplace with programs to address addiction and codependency, family assistance	Operate under a holistic paradigm recognizing the mind-body connection; ensure health and well-being of all
ENVIRONMENTAL ORIENTATION			
The Earth	A "gigantic toolshed"	A source of materials worthy of care and protection	A living presence (Gaia) and major corporate stakeholder
Economics and Ecology	Antagonistic	Connected	Integrated; operations are consistent with ecological laws
Resource Use	Consumption as a way to boost economic prosperity; self-preservation the highest priority	Values of unlimited consumption questioned; focus on sustainability, the sanctity of life, conservation	Focus on integration of life and fulfillment of purpose, recognition of all living systems, preservation
Environmental Protection	A problem; little or no stewardship for the commons accepted	A challenge; shared responsibility for stewardship of the commons	A way of life; no distinction between the commons and personal property
Opportunities in Environmentalism	Few recognized	Economic potential recognized; initial ventures undertaken	New industries developed (Sunrise Seven); old industries reconfigured to incorporate 4 Rs

continues

		Second Wave	Third Wave	Fourth Wave
TECHNOLOGY DEVELOPMENT	Development	In a vacuum	In growing harmony with sociocultural, political, and environmental values	In full accordance with the principles of appropriate technology
	Creativity and Innovation	Dampened by organizational structure	Stimulated by a growing dependence on intuitive techniques and a team-value structure	Maximized by a full marriage of intuition and the rational mind
	Choice of Options	Act without awareness from unconscious scripts	Growing awareness of the need for acting with intent	Primacy of the mind and the centrality of intention recognized
	Assessment	No corporate forum	Corporations establish offices of technology assessment	Corporations assume a leadership role in technology assessment
	Role of Ethics	Little or none	Ethicists employed to consider implications of technologies and corporate actions	Ethical concerns integrated with all aspects of corporate life
LEADERSHIP	Activity	Politics	Aware of need for biopolitics	Biopolitics

Selection of Leaders	Appointment by corporate governing board	Top executives appointed by board; team leaders selected by team members	Through process of multiple, successive elections
Allegiance	Corporate and national	Moving beyond corporate and national boundaries to embrace the Earth and its peoples	Corporate and planetary
Responsibilities	Lead corporation	Lead corporation and contribute to public dialogues on societal and global welfare	Lead corporation, help create global political order, guide and influence public dialogue
Performance Review of Leaders	By governing board; bottom line is main criterion	By governing board; contributions beyond bottom line and outside corporate walls taken into account	By a global council representing all peoples; results of biopolitical activity a major criterion

Suggested Readings

FOR THOSE WHO MAY BE INTERESTED in exploring the ideas we present, the following books have been selected from among the hundreds read as background for the book. Some were a prime source for our ideas; others amplify an argument we presented; and still others have the ability to inspire, provoke strong reactions, or give other perspectives on the issues discussed.

A Changing World

Harman, Willis. 1988. *Global Mind Change: The Promise of the Last Years of the Twentieth Century*. Indianapolis, Ind.: Knowledge Systems.

> A survey of the many ways people are reperceiving cultural, social, intellectual, economic, and political reality. If you have time to read only one book, this should be it.

Land, George, and Beth Jarman. 1992. *Breakpoint and Beyond: Mastering the Future Today*. New York: HarperCollins.

> A noted futurist and corporate consultant translate into business terms the model of biological growth presented in Land's earlier book *Grow or Die*, and explain why business and social leaders should not extrapolate from current trends and conditions in their planning for the future.

Ohmae, Kenichi. 1990. *The Borderless World: Power and Strategy in the Interlinked Economy*. New York: Harper & Row.

> A succinct argument for eliminating nation states and moving beyond nationalism. The author offers numerous examples of how our global economy is interlinked and how trade wars, protectionism, and cries of "buy American" have become nonsensical.

World Commission on Environment and Development. 1987. *Our Common Future*. New York: Oxford University Press.

Also known as the Brundtland report, this book reinforces Ohmae's argument in *The Borderless World* and provides a cogent statement of how countries of the North and South must work together.

Emergence of the Fourth Wave

Alexander, Thea. 1976. *2150*. New York: Warner.

A thoughtful and imaginative novel that explores how different life might be 150 years hence.

Tart, Charles. 1987. *Waking Up: Overcoming the Obstacles to Human Potential*. Boston: Shambhala.

This book introduces both the concept of "consensus trance" and the philosophy of G. I. Gurdjieff, the Russian mystic. The author is one of the few academic psychologists in the United States with an open-minded curiosity about ESP, parapsychology, out-of-body and near-death experiences, and other phenomena beyond the bounds of conventional psychological research.

Toffler, Alvin. 1980. *The Third Wave*. New York: Morrow.

Although written over a decade ago, Toffler's insightful synthesis of a wide variety of trends remains a durable and relevant resource. It is likely that this book will become an indispensable guide for gaining a firmer footing in our era of "socioquakes."

Global Stewardship

Barnet, Richard, and Ronald Muller. 1974. *Global Reach: The Power of the Multinational Corporations*. New York: Simon & Schuster.

A succinct and unflattering picture of the immense range and global power of the major multinational corporations. The reader gains a sense of how nearly twenty years of social, economic, and political forces have altered the multinationals and their culture, habits, and influence.

Brown, Robert McAfee. 1981. *Making Peace in the Global Village*. Philadelphia: Westminster Press.

The author, a Protestant minister, links peacemaking with Christian ethical obligations to help the needy. Though the end of the Cold War has dated some of Brown's allusions, his overall argument—to create true peace we must end the "structural violence" (hunger, homeless-ness, social injustice, and so on) suffered by millions around the world—remains valid.

Harman, Willis. 1979. *An Incomplete Guide to the Future.* New York: Norton.

Anticipates the emergence of "transindustrial" society and suggests ways to smooth the transition to it.

Harman, Willis, and John Hormann. 1990. *Creative Work: The Constructive Role of Business in a Transforming Society.* Indianapolis, Ind.: Knowledge Systems.

Addresses how business can play a positive and valuable role in easing the shift now occurring in global society, and reviews viable social, economic, and cultural movements from our American heritage that we can draw on for guidance in this time of transition.

Naisbitt, John, and Patricia Aburdene. 1985. *Reinventing the Corporation.* New York: Warner.

A prescient view of how trends in global culture are affecting American business.

Redefining Corporate Wealth

Ekins, Paul, ed. 1986. *The Living Economy: A New Economics in the Making.* London: Routledge & Kegan Paul.

An anthology of articles by some of the world's leading alternative economists, including Hazel Henderson, Manfred Max-Neff, Herman Daly, and Johan Galtung, who explore features of new paradigm economics.

Lutz, Mark, and Kenneth Lux. 1979. *The Challenge of Humanistic Economics.* Menlo Park, Calif.: Benjamin-Cummings.

A pioneering effort to rethink mainstream economics by applying the principles of humanistic psychology.

Schumacher, E. F. 1973. *Small Is Beautiful: Economics As If People Mattered.* New York: Harper & Row.

The classic statement of alternative economics and something of a bible for adherents of the living economy. Two short books, *A Guide for the Perplexed* (1978) and *Good Work* (1979), elaborate ideas first presented in *Small Is Beautiful* and offer ethical statements that call us back to the verities of the Christian humanistic tradition while looking ahead to a future where economic systems allow for the integration of these eternal truths.

Corporate Structure

Bezold, Clement, ed. 1978. *Anticipatory Democracy: People in the Politics of the Future*. New York: Random House.

An anthology of writings by a group of politicians, academics, and social analysts. Some contributions anticipate the rise of workplace democracy; articles on technology, participatory management, future economic democracy, and citizen movements are especially valuable.

Senge, Peter. 1990. *The Fifth Discipline: The Art and Practice of the Learning Organization*. New York: Doubleday.

A call for corporations to become learning organizations, in part by applying the principles of general systems theory, by one of the contemporary gurus of American business management.

Vanek, Jaroslav, ed. 1975. *Self-Management: Economic Liberation of Man*. Baltimore: Penguin.

This anthology offers insight on the operation of economic democracy in European factories, particularly in Spain and Yugoslavia. Although the political and ethnic unraveling of Yugoslavia has dated some of the articles, the principles discussed remain persuasive.

Zwerdling, Daniel. 1980. *Workplace Democracy: A Guide to Workplace Ownership, Participation and Self-Management Experiments in the United States*. New York: Harper & Row.

A source of examples on how contemporary businesses have used democratic principles in manufacturing settings, this book also reviews Spain's Mondragon system of cooperatives and turns a critical eye on ESOPs.

Community

Peck, M. Scott. 1987. *The Different Drum: Community Making and Peace*. New York: Simon & Schuster.

Part autobiography, part advocacy and guidance for embarking on the community-building process, this book offers a vivid image of the rewards that accrue when people interact "in community." At the same time, it conveys the difficulty of creating a true community.

Sale, Kirkpatrick. 1980. *Human Scale*. New York: Coward, McCann & Geoghegan.

A cogent argument on the need for social, political, and economic systems to be scaled down and reconstituted in forms we can relate to and in sizes that foster the formation of community.

Schaef, Anne Wilson. 1985. *Women's Reality: An Emerging Female System in a White Male Society*. New York: Harper & Row.

One of the few books to delineate clearly the difference in perception between men and women. The author provides a wealth of clues on how the feminization of our culture is changing our view of reality.

Schaef, Anne Wilson, and Diane Fassel. 1988. *The Addictive Organization*. New York: Harper & Row.

Extends a therapeutic model to corporate America to argue that addictive patterns of thinking and living are manifest in relations between workers and managers and between customers and employees, and that these patterns contribute to a pervasive social pathology.

Ecology and Economics

Devall, Bill, and George Sessions. 1985. *Deep Ecology*. Salt Lake City, Utah: G. M. Smith.

Links the environmental and spirituality movements; excellent appendices contain seminal articles that laid the groundwork for the deep ecology movement.

Elgin, Duane. 1981. *Voluntary Simplicity: Toward a Way of Life That Is Outwardly Simple, Inwardly Rich*. New York: Morrow.

Both reports the social trend toward simplifying lifestyles and advocates such a shift.

Leopold, Aldo. 1966. *A Sand County Almanac*. New York: Ballantine.

A nonfiction classic by an American naturalist with a fine eye for nature and the eloquence to capture his vision in words. The section on the land ethic has become a key element in contemporary environmental and ethical thinking.

Pitt, D. C., ed. 1988. *The Future of the Environment: The Social Dimensions of Conservation and Ecological Alternatives*. London: Routledge.

In this pioneering work, the author explores the social implications of the environmental movement and relates ecology to the new international economic order and the concept of structural violence.

Shepard, Paul, and Daniel McKinley, eds. 1969. *The Subversive Science: Essays Toward an Ecology of Man*. Boston: Houghton Mifflin.

Articles in this anthology illustrate the challenge ecology presents to conventional thinking in economics, demography, philosophy, theology, ethics, and male-female relationships.

Appropriate Technology

Congdon, R. J., ed. 1977. *Introduction to Appropriate Technology: Toward a Simpler Lifestyle*. Emmaus, Pa.: Rodale.

As much a practical guide as a theoretical exposition, this anthology sets out criteria for appropriate technology and then shows it at work in various Third World countries.

Rifkin, Jeremy. 1983. *Algeny: A New Word, A New World*. New York: Viking.

A widely read, though debatable, diatribe against the indiscriminate development and application of biotechnology that is valuable for raising key questions that we, as a society, have barely begun to try to answer.

Winner, Langdon. 1977. *Autonomous Technology*. Cambridge, Mass.: MIT Press.

A thoughtful treatment of the theme of technology as an autonomous force in our culture.

Biopolitics

Anderson, Walter T. 1987. *To Govern Evolution: Further Adventures of the Political Animal*. New York: Harcourt Brace Jovanovich.

A study of the implications of modern biology and environmental awareness that focuses on how we might retrain and prepare ourselves to "govern evolution."

Russell, Peter, and Roger Evans. 1992. *The Creative Manager: Finding Inner Vision and Wisdom in Uncertain Times*. San Francisco: Jossey-Bass.

Offers an image of the qualities and abilities, particularly the new mental habits and ways of perceiving reality, that will characterize the successful manager of the future.

Satin, Mark. 1979. *New Age Politics: Healing Self and Society*. New York: Delta.

Relates "New Age" principles about personal empowerment to the political process in order to reconceive contemporary political issues like racism, ethics, local government, and voting. The author demonstrates that much in the New Age movement is not really new at all but draws on ancient and venerable roots.

Spretnak, Charlene, and Fritjof Capra. 1986. *Green Politics*. Santa Fe, N. Mex.: Bear & Co.

A study of the principles and philosophy of the German "green" political movement, with an assessment of their applicability to the U.S. political system.

Bibliography

Adams, John, ed. 1984. *Transforming Work*. Alexandria, Va.: Miles River Press.

———, ed. 1986. *Transforming Leadership: From Vision to Results*. Alexandria, Va.: Miles River Press

Adams, John, and Sabina Spencer. 1986. "Introduction: The Strategic Leadership Perspective." In *Transforming Leadership*, edited by John Adams. Alexandria, Va: Miles River Press.

Adelman, Irma, and Cynthia Taft Morris. 1973. *Economic Growth and Social Equity in Developing Countries*. Stanford, Calif.: Stanford University Press.

Adizes, Ichak. 1975. "A Typology of Various Experiments in the World and a Discussion of the Role of Professional Management." In *Self-Management*, edited by Ichak Adizes and Elisabeth Borgese. Santa Barbara, Calif.: ABC-Clio.

Adizes, Ichak, and Elisabeth Borgese, eds. 1975. *Self-Management: New Dimensions to Democracy*. Santa Barbara, Calif.: ABC-Clio.

Adlestein, Michael, and Jean Pival, eds. 1972. *Women's Liberation: Perspectives*. New York: St. Martin's Press.

Agor, Weston. 1984. *Intuitive Management: Integrating Left and Right Brain Management Skills*. Englewood Cliffs, N.J.: Prentice Hall.

———. 1986. *The Logic of Intuitive Decision Making*. New York: Quorum Books.

Alexander, Thea. 1976. *2150*. New York: Warner.

Allen, F. 1992. "U.S. Companies Plan Alliance on Recycling." *Wall Street Journal*, September 14, A3, A7.

"An American Vision for the 1990s." *Fortune*, March 26, 1990.

Anders, Gigi. 1990. "Personalities." *The Washington Post*, May 28, B3.

Anderson, Walter T. 1983. *The Upstart Spring*. Reading, Mass.: Addison-Wesley.

———. 1986. "The Pitfalls of Bioregionalism." *Utne Reader*, February/March.

————. 1987. *To Govern Evolution: Further Adventures of the Political Animal.* New York: Harcourt Brace Jovanich.

Arenson, Karen. 1991. "The Boss: Underworked and Overpaid?" *The New York Times Book Review*, November 17.

Ashkenas, Ronald, and Robert Schaffer. 1992. "The Lemmings Who Love Quality." *The New York Times*, May 3.

AtKisson, Alan. 1991a. "Beyond Bureaucracy: The Development Agenda." *In Context*, April.

————. 1991b. "Postmodern Politics." *In Context*, Fall/Winter.

Augros, Robert, and George Stanciu. 1984. *The New Story of Science.* New York: Bantam.

Autry, James. 1991. *Love and Profit: The Art of Caring Leadership.* New York: Morrow.

Baker, David. 1978. "State, Regional and Local Experiments in Anticipatory Democracy: An Overview." In *Anticipatory Democracy*, edited by Clement Bezold. New York: Random House.

Barbour, Ian, ed. 1973. *Western Man and Environmental Ethics: Attitudes Toward Nature and Technology.* Menlo Park, Calif.: Addison-Wesley.

Barnet, Richard. 1980. *The Lean Years: Politics in the Age of Scarcity.* New York: Simon & Schuster.

Barnet, Richard, and Ronald Muller. 1974. *Global Reach: The Power of the Multinational Corporations.* New York: Simon & Schuster.

Bartlett, John. 1968. *Familiar Quotations.* Boston: Little, Brown.

Bateson, Gregory. 1987. *Steps to an Ecology of Mind.* Northvale, N.J.: Jason Aronson.

"The Battle for Control—Getting Smart and Making Changes." *Inferential Focus Briefing,* February 20, 1992.

Bellah, Robert N. 1989. "A Hot Streak for Democracy." *The New York Times Book Review*, November 12.

Bellah, Robert N., Richard Madsen, William M. Sullivan, Ann Swidler, and Steven M. Tipton. 1985. *Habits of the Heart.* New York: Harper & Row.

————. 1991. *The Good Society.* New York: Knopf.

Bellas, C. J. 1975. "Industrial Democracy Through Worker Ownership: An American Experience." In *Self-Management*, edited by Jaroslav Vanek. Baltimore: Penguin.

Bender, Tom. 1978a. "Appropriate Technology and Resources." In *Appropriate Visions*, edited by Richard Dorf and Yvonne Hunter. San Francisco: Boyd & Fraser.

———. 1978b. "New Values." In *Stepping Stones*, edited by Lane de Moll and Gigi Coe. New York: Schocken.

———. 1978c. "Why Big Business Loves A.T." In *Stepping Stones*, edited by Lane de Moll and Gigi Coe. New York: Schocken.

Benello, C. George. 1978. "Economic Democracy and the Future: The Unfinished Task." In *Anticipatory Democracy*, edited by Clement Bezold. New York: Random House.

Bennett, Amanda. 1991. "Making the Grade with the Customer." *Wall Street Journal*.

Bennis, Warren. 1989. *On Becoming a Leader*. Reading, Mass.: Addison-Wesley.

Benson, Herbert. 1980. *The Mind/Body Effect*. New York: Berkley.

Berg, Ivar. 1974. "Worker Discontent, Humanistic Management and Repetitious History." In *Humanizing the Workplace*, edited by Roy Fairfield. Buffalo, N.Y.: Prometheus Books.

Berg, Peter, ed. 1978. *Reinhabiting a Separate Country: A Bioregional Anthology*. San Francisco: Planet Drum Foundation.

Berg, Peter, and Raymond Dasmann. 1978. "Reinhabiting California." In *Reinhabiting a Separate Country*, edited by Peter Berg. San Francisco: Planet Drum Foundation.

Bergland, Richard. 1985. *The Fabric of Mind*. New York: Viking.

Berle, A. A., Jr. 1971. "What GNP Doesn't Tell Us." In *Global Ecology*, edited by John Holdren and Paul Ehrlich. New York: Harcourt Brace Jovanovich.

Berman, Morris. 1981. *The Reenchantment of the World*. Ithaca, N.Y.: Cornell University Press.

Berry, Thomas. 1988. *The Dream of the Earth*. San Francisco: Sierra Club Books.

Berry, Wendell. 1973. "A Secular Pilgrimage." In *Western Man and Environmental Ethics*, edited by Ian Barbour. Menlo Park, Calif.: Addison-Wesley.

———. 1976. "Where Cities and Farms Come Together." In *Radical Agriculture*, edited by Richard Merrill. New York: New York University Press.

———. 1977. *The Unsettling of America: Culture and Agriculture*. San Francisco: Sierra Club Books.

————. 1978. "Horsedrawn Tools and the Doctrine of Labor Saving." In *Stepping Stones*, edited by Lane de Moll and Gigi Coe. New York: Schocken.

Bezold, Clement, ed. 1978a. *Anticipatory Democracy: People in the Politics of the Future*. New York: Random House.

————. 1978b. "Lucas Aerospace: The Workers' Plan for Socially Useful Products." In *Anticipatory Democracy*, edited by Clement Bezold. New York: Random House.

Bezold, Clement, Rick Carlson, and Jonathan Peck. 1986. *The Future of Work and Health*. Dover, Mass.: Auburn House.

Bloch, Barbara. 1990. "Intuition Creeps Out of the Closet and into the Boardroom." *Management Review*, May.

Bluestone, Irving. 1974. "Worker Participation in Decision Making." In *Humanizing the Workplace*, edited by Roy Fairfield. Buffalo, N.Y.: Prometheus Books.

Blumenthal, Sidney, and James Chace. 1992. "Memo to the Democrats." *The New York Times*, February 23.

Boeing Co. 1992. "Higher Order Technology." *The New York Times*, May 13.

Bookchin, Murray. 1976. "Radical Agriculture." In *Radical Agriculture*, edited by Richard Merrill. New York: New York University Press.

————. 1978. "From *Towards a Liberatory Technology*." In *Stepping Stones*, edited by Lane de Moll and Gigi Coe. New York: Schocken.

Borsodi, Ralph. 1922. *The New Accounting: Bookkeeping Without Books of Original Entry by the Use of a Natural System of Double Entry Bookkeeping*. New York: Dodd, Mead.

————. 1927. *The Distribution Age: A Study of the Economy of Modern Distribution*. New York: Appleton.

————. 1929. *This Ugly Civilization*. New York: Simon & Schuster.

————. 1933. *Flight from the City: The Story of a New Way to Family Security*. New York: Harper & Brothers.

————. 1948. *Education and Living*. Suffern, N.Y.: The School of Living.

Botkin, James, Mahdi Elmandjra, and Mircea Malitza. 1979. *No Limits to Learning: Bridging the Human Gap—A Report to the Club of Rome*. New York: Pergamon.

Boulding, Kenneth. 1970. "Economics of the Coming Spaceship Earth." In *The Environmental Handbook*, edited by Garrett de Bell. New York: Ballantine.

————. 1978. *Ecodynamics: A New Theory of Societal Evolution*. London: Sage.

————. 1980. "Spaceship Earth Revisited." In *Economics, Ecology, and Ethics*, edited by Herman Daly. San Francisco: W. H. Freeman.

Brandt, Willy. 1980. *North-South: A Programme for Survival*. Cambridge, Mass.: MIT Press.

Breslaw, John. 1970. "Economics and Ecosystems." In *The Environmental Handbook*, edited by Garrett de Bell. New York: Ballantine.

Brown, Robert McAfee. 1981. *Making Peace in the Global Village*. Philadelphia: Westminster Press.

Brustein, Robert. 1990. "Speaking Truth to Power." *The New York Times Book Review*, June 17.

Buckley, Karen Wilhelm, and Dani Perkins. 1984. "Managing the Complexity of Organizational Transformation." In *Transforming Work*, edited by John Adams. Alexandria, Va.: Miles River Press.

Buckley, Karen Wilhelm, and Joan Steffy. 1986. "The Invisible Side of Leadership." In *Transforming Leadership*, edited by John Adams. Alexandria, Va.: Miles River Press.

Burton, John. 1990. *Conflict: Resolution and Prevention*. New York: St. Martin's Press.

Cadman, David. 1986. "Money as if People Mattered." In *The Living Economy*, edited by Paul Ekins. London: Routledge & Kegan Paul.

Capra, Fritjof. 1975. *The Tao of Physics*. Boston: Shambhala

————. 1982. *The Turning Point: Science, Society and the Rising Culture*. New York: Bantam.

Carey, Kenneth. 1982. *The Starseed Transmission*. Kansas City, Mo.: Uni-Sun.

Carlzon, Jan. 1987. *Moments of Truth*. New York: Ballinger.

Carroll, James. 1973. "Participatory Technology." In *Western Man and Environmental Ethics*, edited by Ian Barbour. Menlo Park, Calif.: Addison-Wesley.

Carson, Rachel. 1962. *Silent Spring*. Greenwich, Conn.: Fawcett Crest.

Catton, William R, Jr. 1980. *Overshoot: The Ecological Basis of Revolutionary Change*. Urbana: University of Illinois Press.

Cetron, Marvin, and Owen Davies. 1989. *American Renaissance: Our Life at the Turn of the 21st Century*. New York: St. Martin's Press.

Chambers, R. 1988. "Putting People First. " In *The Future of the Environment*, edited by D. C. Pitt. London: Routledge.

Chemical Bank. 1992a. "Be Innovative, or Begone." *The New York Times*, May 13.

————. 1992b. "With Intellectual Currency Capital Strength Is More than Just Money in the Bank." *The New York Times*, March 19.

Chion-Kenney, Linda. 1990. "The 'Cold Evil'? Taking Global Responsibility Personally." *The Washington Post*, April 6.

Cleveland, Harlan. 1985. *The Knowledge Executive: Leadership in an Information Society*. New York: Dutton.

Clinton, William. 1992. "Transcript of Acceptance Speech." *The New York Times*, July 17.

Cobb, John, Jr. 1972. *Is It Too Late? A Theology of Ecology*. Beverly Hills, Calif.: Bruce.

Coke, Alfred, and Michael Mierau. 1984. "A Formula for Corporate Fitness." In *Transforming Work*, edited by John Adams. Alexandria, Va.: Miles River Press.

Coleman, John. 1978. "Ethics and Intermediate Technology." In *Appropriate Visions*, edited by Richard Dorf and Yvonne Hunter. San Francisco: Boyd & Fraser.

Collard, David. 1978. *Altruism and Economy: A Study in Non-Selfish Economics*. Oxford, England: Martin Robertson.

Columbia Business School. 1992. "How AT&T Invests in Its Key Asset: Brainpower." *The New York Times*, January 23.

Commission on Population Growth and the American Future. 1972. *Population and the American Future*. New York: New American Library.

Commoner, Barry. 1971. *The Closing Circle: Nature, Man and Technology*. New York: Knopf.

————. 1974. "A Healthy Environment." In *Earthkeeping*, edited by Susan Mehrtens and Charles Juzek. Pacific Grove, Calif.: Boxwood Press.

Congdon, R. J., ed. 1977. *Introduction to Appropriate Technology: Toward a Simpler Lifestyle*. Emmaus, Pa.: Rodale Press.

Conover, Donald. 1978. "The Case for Participatory Management." In *Anticipatory Democracy*, edited by Clement Bezold. New York: Random House.

Cook, Brian. 1991. "Quality: The Pioneers Survey the Landscape." *Industry Week*, October 21.

Cook, Earl. 1980. "Limits to Exploitation of Non-Renewable Resources." In *Economics, Ecology, and Ethics*, edited by Herman Daly. San Francisco: W. H. Freeman.

Corbet, Hugh, and Robert Jackson, eds. 1974. *In Search of a New World Economic Order*. London: Croom Helm.

Covey, Stephen. 1989. *The Seven Habits of Highly Effective People*. New York: Simon & Schuster.

Cox, Craig. 1991. "The Listening Corporation." *Business Ethics*, November/December.

Cox, Craig, and Sally Power. 1992. "Executives of the World Unite!" *Business Ethics*, September/October.

Crystal, Graef. 1991. *In Search of Excess: The Overcompensation of American Executives*. New York: Norton.

Curzon, Gerard. 1974. "Crisis in the International Trading System." In *In Search of a New World Economic Order*, edited by Hugh Corbet and Robert Jackson. London: Croom Helm.

Daly, Herman. 1973a. "The Steady-State Economy: Toward a Political Economy of Biophysical Equilibrium and Moral Growth." In *Toward a Steady-State Economy*, edited by Herman Daly. San Francisco: W. H. Freeman.

———, ed. 1973b. *Toward a Steady-State Economy*. San Francisco: W. H. Freeman.

———. 1977. *Steady-State Economics: The Economics of Biophysical Equilibrium and Moral Growth*. San Francisco: W. H. Freeman.

———, ed. 1980a. *Economics, Ecology, and Ethics: Essays Toward a Steady-State Economy*. San Francisco: W. H. Freeman.

———. 1980b. "On Economics as a Life Science." In *Economics, Ecology, and Ethics*, edited by Herman Daly. San Francisco: W. H. Freeman.

———. 1980c. "Postscript: Some Common Misunderstandings and Further Issues Concerning a Steady-State Economy. In *Economics, Ecology, and Ethics*, edited by Herman Daly. San Francisco: W. H. Freeman.

———. 1988. "Moving to a Steady State Economy." In *The Cassandra Conference*, edited by Paul Ehrlich and John Holdren. College Station: Texas A&M University Press.

Daly, Herman, and Harford Thomas. 1986. "The Reality of a Finite Planet." In *The Living Economy*, edited by Paul Ekins. London: Routledge & Kegan Paul.

Damgaard, Jacqueline. 1987. "The Inner Self-Helper: Transcendent Life Within Life?" In *Consciousness and Survival*, edited by J. Spong. Sausalito, Calif.: Institute of Noetic Sciences.

Dator, James. 1978. "The Future of Anticipatory Democracy." In *Anticipatory Democracy*, edited by Clement Bezold. New York: Random House.

Dauncey, Guy. 1986. "A New Local Economic Order." In *The Living Economy*, edited by Paul Ekins. London: Routledge & Kegan Paul.

Davis, Stanley. 1987. *Future Perfect*. Reading, Mass.: Addison-Wesley.

"A Day to Take Our Daughters to Work." *Parade*, May 17, 1992.

de Bell, Garrett, ed. 1970a. *The Environmental Handbook*. New York: Ballantine.

de Bell, Garrett. 1970b. "A Future That Makes Ecological Sense." In *The Environmental Handbook*, edited by Garrett de Bell. New York: Ballantine.

―――. 1970c. "Recycling." In *The Environmental Handbook*, edited by Garrett de Bell. New York: Ballantine.

de Moll, Lane, and Gigi Coe, eds. 1978. *Stepping Stones: Appropriate Technology and Beyond*. New York: Schocken.

Denman, Clayton. 1978. "Small Towns Are the Future of America." In *Humanscape*, edited by Stephen Kaplan and Rachel Kaplan. Boston: Duxbury Press.

De Pree, Max. 1989. *Leadership Is an Art*. New York: Doubleday.

Derr, Thomas. 1975. *Ecology and Human Need*. Philadelphia: Westminster Press.

Deutsch, Claudia. 1991. "Call It 'C.E.O. Disease,' Then Listen." *The New York Times*, December 15.

Devall, Bill, and George Sessions. 1985. *Deep Ecology*. Salt Lake City, Utah: G. M. Smith.

de Wilde, Tom. 1977. "Some Social Criteria for Appropriate Technology." In *Introduction to Appropriate Technology*, edited by R. J. Congdon. Emmaus, Pa.: Rodale Press.

Dickinson, Harry. 1977. "The Transfer of Knowledge and the Adoption of Technologies." In *Introduction to Appropriate Technology*, edited by R. J. Congdon. Emmaus, Pa.: Rodale Press.

Dorf, Richard, and Yvonne Hunter, eds. 1978. *Appropriate Visions: Technology, the Environment and the Individual*. San Francisco: Boyd & Fraser.

Dossey, Larry. 1982. *Space, Time and Medicine*. Boston: Shambhala.

Doyal, Len, and Ian Gough. 1986. "Human Need and Strategies for Social Change." In *The Living Economy*, edited by Paul Ekins. London: Routledge & Kegan Paul.

Dubos, Rene. 1970. "The Limits of Adaptability." In *The Environmental Handbook*, edited by Garrett de Bell. New York: Ballantine.

―――. 1980. *The Wooing of the Earth*. New York: Charles Scribner's Sons.

Dychtwald, Ken. 1989. *Age Wave: The Challenges and Opportunities of an Aging America*. Los Angeles: Tarcher.

Eccles, John, and Karl Popper. 1977. *The Self and Its Brain*. Boston: Routledge & Kegan Paul.

Eddington, A. S. 1929. *The Nature of the Physical World*. New York: Macmillan.

Ehrenfeld, David. 1978. *The Arrogance of Humanism*. New York: Oxford University Press.

Ehrlich, Paul. 1971. "Looking Backward from 2000 A.D." In *Global Ecology*, edited by John Holdren and Paul Ehrlich. New York: Harcourt Brace Jovanovich.

———. 1972. *Population, Resources, Environment*. San Francisco: W. H. Freeman.

Ehrlich, Paul, and Anne Ehrlich. 1974. *The End of Affluence: A Blueprint for Your Future*. New York: Ballantine.

Ehrlich, Paul, and John Holdren, eds. 1988. *The Cassandra Conference: Resources and the Human Predicament*. College Station: Texas A&M University Press.

Ekins, Paul. 1986a. "Co-operation: Where the Social Meets the Economic." In *The Living Economy*, edited by Paul Ekins. London: Routledge & Kegan Paul.

———, ed. 1986b. *The Living Economy: A New Economics in the Making*. London: Routledge & Kegan Paul.

Elgin, Duane. 1981. *Voluntary Simplicity: Toward a Way of Life That Is Outwardly Simple, Inwardly Rich*. New York: Morrow.

Elkington, John. 1986. "The Sunrise Seven." In *The Living Economy*, edited by Paul Ekins. London: Routledge & Kegan Paul.

Ellenberger, Henri. 1970. *The Discovery of the Unconscious*. New York: Basic Books.

Ellerman, D. 1975. "Capitalism and Workers' Self-Management." In *Self-Management*, edited by Jaroslav Vanek. Baltimore: Penguin.

Elliott, Margaret. 1990. "The Death of the Organization Man." *The New York Times Book Review*, March 18.

Elliott, Stuart. 1992. "In Nynex's New Campaign, It's People Over Machines." *The New York Times*, January 23.

Engel, R. 1988. "Ethics." In *The Future of the Environment*, edited by D. C. Pitt. London: Routledge & Kegan Paul.

Euler, Lee. 1992. "21 Remarkable Forecasts for 1992–93." *Financial Predictions*, Spring.

"Executive Transformation and Personal Paradigm Shifts." *The New Leaders*, May/June 1991.

Fairfield, Roy, ed. 1974. *Humanizing the Workplace*. Buffalo, N.Y.: Prometheus Books.

Falk, Richard. 1973. "Reforming World Order: Zones of Consciousness and Domains of Action." In *The World System*, edited by Ervin Laszlo. New York: Braziller.

———. 1987. "Transition to Peace and Justice: The Challenge of Transcendence Without Utopia." In *Global Peace and Security*, edited by Wolfram Hanrieder. Boulder, Colo.: Westview Press.

Fassel, Diane. 1990. *Working Ourselves to Death*. San Francisco: Harper.

Fein, Mitchell. 1974. "The Myth of Job Enrichment." In *Humanizing the Workplace*, edited by Roy Fairfield. Buffalo, N.Y.: Prometheus Books.

Ferguson, Kathy. 1984. *The Feminist Case Against Bureaucracy*. Philadelphia: Temple University Press.

Ferguson, Marilyn. 1980. *The Aquarian Conspiracy: Personal and Social Transformation in Our Time*. Los Angeles: Tarcher.

Fischer, Ruth. 1975. "Black, Female and Qualified." In *Women on Campus*. New Rochelle, N.Y.: Change Magazine.

Fisher, Lawrence. 1992. "Patents: Aggressive Defender Branches Out." *The New York Times*, January 25.

Forest, Lila. 1991. "Discovering Public Life." *In Context*, Fall/Winter.

Fowler, Elizabeth. 1992. "Stepping Up the Training in Ecology." *The New York Times*, March 17.

Friedman, Milton. 1970. "The Social Responsibility of Business Is to Increase Its Profits." *The New York Times Magazine*, September 13.

Friend, Gil. 1978. "Nurturing a Responsible Agriculture." In *Stepping Stones*, edited by Lane de Moll and Gigi Coe. New York: Schocken.

Fritz, Robert. 1986. "The Leader as Creator." In *Transforming Leadership*, edited by John Adams. Alexandria, Va.: Miles River Press.

———. 1989. *The Path of Least Resistance: Learning to Become the Creative Force in Your Own Life*. New York: Ballantine.

Fuller, Buckminster. 1975. *Synergetics: Explorations in the Geometry of Thinking*. New York: Collier Books.

———. 1981a. "Birthday Celebration." *The New York Times*, July 7.

————. 1981b. *Critical Path*. New York: St. Martin's Press.

Galagan, Patricia. 1989. "Growth: Mapping Its Patterns and Periods." *Training and Development Journal*, November.

Galtung, Johan. 1969. 1975–1980. *Essays in Peace Research*. (5 vols.) Copenhagen: Christean Ejlers.

————. 1986. "Toward a New Economics: On the Theory and Practice of Self-Reliance." In *The Living Economy*, edited by Paul Ekins. London: Routledge & Kegan Paul.

————. 1987. "On the Rise of the Fourth World." In *Global Peace and Security*, edited by Wolfram Hanrieder. Boulder, Colo.: Westview Press.

————. 1988. "The Green Movement." In *The Future of the Environment*, edited by D. C. Pitt. London: Routledge & Kegan Paul.

Gardels, Nathan. 1989. "The Greening of International Affairs." *San Francisco Chronicle*, April 12, B1.

Garrett, Roger. 1978. "Good Engineering Produces Appropriate Technology." In *Appropriate Visions*, edited by Richard Dorf and Yvonne Hunter. San Francisco: Boyd & Fraser.

Garson, G. D. 1975. "Recent Developments in Workers' Participation in Europe." In *Self-Management*, edited by Jaroslav Vanek. Baltimore: Penguin.

Gaylin, Willard. 1990. *Adam and Eve and Pinocchio: On Being and Becoming Human*. New York: Viking.

Geiser, B. K. 1991. "The Greening of Industry." *Technology Review*, August/September.

Gelb, Leslie. 1991. "Fresh Face." *The New York Times Magazine*, December 8.

George, Susan. 1986. "The Debt Crisis." In *The Living Economy*, edited by Paul Ekins. London: Routledge & Kegan Paul.

Georgescu-Roegen, Nicholas. 1980. "The Entropy Law and the Economic Problem." In *Economics, Ecology, and Ethics*, edited by Herman Daly. San Francisco: W. H. Freeman.

Gilliam, Harold. 1989. "Greening Begins at Home." *San Francisco Chronicle*, March 12, 18.

Gillingham, Peter. 1978. "Appropriate Agriculture." In *Appropriate Visions*, edited by Richard Dorf and Yvonne Hunter. San Francisco: Boyd & Fraser.

"Golden Age Near, Michigan Scholars Are Told." *The New York Times*, May 3, 1992.

Goleman, Daniel. 1985. *Vital Lies, Simple Truths*. New York: Simon & Schuster.

Goodman, Paul. 1973. "Can Technology Be Humane?" In *Western Man and Environmental Ethics*, edited by Ian Barbour. Menlo Park, Calif.: Addison-Wesley.

Gozdz, Kazimierz. 1993. "Building Community as a Leadership Discipline." In *The New Paradigm in Business: Emerging Strategies for Leadership and Organizational Change*, edited by Michael Ray and Alan Rinzler. Los Angeles: Tarcher/Perigee.

Greenewalt, Crawford. 1959. *The Uncommon Man: The Individual in the Organization*. New York: McGraw-Hill.

Greenhouse, Steven. 1990. "In Search of Capitalism with a Human Face." *The New York Times*, May 20.

Gregg, Richard. 1978. "Voluntary Simplicity." In *Stepping Stones*, edited by Lane de Moll and Gigi Coe. New York: Schocken.

Hacker, Andrew. 1990. "Affirmative Action: A Negative Opinion." *The New York Times Book Review*, July 1.

Hagberg, Janet. 1984. *Real Power: Stages of Personal Power in Organizations*. Minneapolis, Minn.: Winston Press.

Hammer, Michael. 1990. "Reengineering Work: Don't Automate, Obliterate." *Harvard Business Review*, July/August.

Hancock, Trevor. 1986. "Health-Based Indicators of Economic Prosperity." *The Living Economy*, edited by Paul Ekins. London: Routledge & Kegan Paul.

Hannon, Bruce. 1980. "Energy Use and Moral Restraint." In *Economics, Ecology, and Ethics*, edited by Herman Daly. San Francisco: W. H. Freeman.

Hardin, Garrett. 1968. "The Tragedy of the Commons." *Science* 162: 1243–1248.

Harman, Willis. 1979. *An Incomplete Guide to the Future*. New York: Norton.

———. 1982. *Changing Belief Systems*. Menlo Park, Calif.: SRI International VALS Report no. 33.

———. 1986a. "The Role of Corporations." In *The Living Economy*, edited by Paul Ekins. London: Routledge & Kegan Paul.

———. 1986b. "Transformed Leadership: Two Contrasting Concepts." In *Transforming Leadership*, edited by John Adams. Alexandria, Va.: Miles River Press.

———. 1988. *Global Mind Change: The Promise of the Last Years of the Twentieth Century*. Indianapolis, Ind.: Knowledge Systems.

———. 1992. "21st-Century Business: A Background for Dialogue." In *New Traditions in Business*, edited by John Renesch. San Francisco: Berrett-Koehler.

Harman, Willis, and John Hormann. 1990. *Creative Work: The Constructive Role of Business in a Transforming Society*. Indianapolis, Ind.: Knowledge Systems.

Harman, Willis, and Howard Rheingold. 1984. *Higher Creativity*. Los Angeles: Tarcher.

Havel, Václav. 1990. "To the Joint Session of the U.S. Congress." *Noetic Sciences Review*, Spring.

Hawken, Paul. 1992. "The Ecology of Commerce." *Inc.*, April.

Hayes, Denis. 1977. *Rays of Hope: The Transition to a Post-Petroleum World*. New York: Norton.

Heider, John. 1985. *The Tao of Leadership: Leadership Strategies for a New Age*. New York: Bantam.

Heisenberg, Werner. 1960. "The Representation of Nature in Contemporary Physics." In *Symbolism in Religion and Literature*, edited by R. May. New York: Braziller.

Henderson, Hazel. 1976. "Citizen Movements for Greater Global Equity." *International Social Science Journal* 28: 773–788.

———. 1978. "Citizen Movements: Charting Alternative Futures." In *Anticipatory Democracy*, edited by Clement Bezold. New York: Random House.

———. 1981. *Politics of the Solar Age*. New York: Doubleday.

Henderson, Hazel, John Lintott, and Paul Sparrow. 1986. "Indicators of No Real Meaning." In *The Living Economy*, edited by Paul Ekins. London: Routledge & Kegan Paul.

Henkoff, Ronald. 1989. "Is Greed Dead?" *Fortune*, August 14.

Hennig, Margaret, and Anne Jardim. 1977. *The Managerial Woman*. New York: Doubleday.

Herman, Ellen, and James Hillman. 1992. "Are Politics and Therapy Compatible?" *Utne Reader*, January/February.

Hodgkinson, Virginia, Richard Lyman, and Associates. 1989. *The Future of the Nonprofit Sector*. San Francisco: Jossey-Bass.

Holdren, John, and Paul Ehrlich, eds. 1971. *Global Ecology: Readings Toward a Rational Strategy for Man*. New York: Harcourt Brace Jovanovich.

Holusha, John. 1992a. "Learning to Wrap Products in Less—Or Nothing at All." *The New York Times*, January 19.

———. 1992b. "Organics Sprout a New Following." *The New York Times*, May 2.

Houston, Jean. 1974. "Myth, Consciousness and Psychic Research." In *Psychic Exploration*, edited by Edgar Mitchel and John White. New York: Putnam.

———. 1988. "Sacred Stewardship." *In Context*, Autumn.

Howe, Louise. 1974. "Women in the Workplace." In *Humanizing the Workplace*, edited by Roy Fairfield. Buffalo, N.Y.: Prometheus Books.

Howe, Marvine. 1992. "Barnard Chief Urges Women to Step into Leadership Roles." *The New York Times*, May 13.

Hueting, Roefie. 1986. "An Economic Scenario for a Conserver-Economy." In *The Living Economy*, edited by Paul Ekins. London: Routledge & Kegan Paul.

Hyams, Edward. 1952. *Soil and Civilization*. New York: Harper & Row.

Ilgen, Thomas. 1987. "Promoting Technology Trade: Strategies for Suppliers and Recipients." In *Global Peace and Security*, edited by Wolfram Hanrieder. Boulder, Colo.: Westview.

Illich, Ivan. 1978. "The Nature of Tools." In *Stepping Stones*, edited by Lane de Moll and Gigi Coe. New York: Schocken.

Jaffe, Dennis, Cynthia Scott, and Esther Orioli. 1986. "Visionary Leadership: Moving a Company from Burnout to Inspired Performance." In *Transforming Leadership*, edited by John Adams. Alexandria, Va.: Miles River Press.

Jahn, Robert, and Brenda Dunne. 1987. *Margins of Reality: The Role of Consciousness in the Physical World*. New York: Harcourt Brace Jovanovich.

Janssen, Peter. 1970. "The Age of Ecology." In *Ecotactics*, edited by John Mitchell. New York: Pocket Books.

Jeans, James. 1943. *Physics and Philosophy*. New York: Dover.

Johnson, Warren. 1979. *Muddling Toward Frugality*. Boston: Shambhala.

———. 1985. *The Future Is Not What It Used to Be: Returning to Traditional Values in an Age of Scarcity*. New York: Dodd, Mead.

Josephson, Brian. 1985. "Conversation." *Nobel Prize Conversations*. San Francisco: Saybrook.

Jung, C. G. 1933. *Modern Man in Search of a Soul*. New York: Harcourt Brace Jovanovich.

———. 1957. *The Undiscovered Self*. New York: New American Library.

———. 1965. *Memories, Dreams, Reflections*. New York: Vintage.

Kaku, Ryuzaburo. 1992. "Perestroika in Japan." *Washington Quarterly*, Summer.

Kaminer, Wendy. 1990. "Chances Are You're Codependent Too." *The New York Times Book Review*, February 11.

Kanter, Rosabeth Moss. 1983. *The Change Masters: Innovations and Entrepreneurship in the American Corporation*. New York: Simon & Schuster.

———. 1987. "Performance Pressure: Life in the Limelight." In *Competition: A Feminist Taboo?* edited by Valerie Miner and Helen Longino. New York: Feminist Press at CUNY.

———. 1990. *When Giants Learn to Dance*. New York: Simon & Schuster.

Kaplan, Stephen, and Rachel Kaplan. 1978. *Humanscape: Environments for People*. Boston: Duxbury Press.

Kelly, Marjorie. 1992. "Interview with Willis Harman." *Business Ethics*, March/April.

Kennard, Byron. 1978. "Tomorrow's Technology: Who Decides?" In *Anticipatory Democracy*, edited by Clement Bezold. New York: Random House.

Kerans, Patrick. 1974. *Sinful Social Structures*. New York: Paulist Press.

Keyes, Ken, Jr. 1983. *The Hundredth Monkey*. Coos Bay, Oreg.: Vision Books.

Kiechel, Walter. 1989. "The Workaholic Generation." *Fortune*, April 10.

———. 1992. "The Leader as Servant." *Fortune*, May 4.

Kiefer, Charles. 1986. "Leadership in Metanoic Organizations." In *Transforming Leadership*, edited by John Adams. Alexandria, Va.: Miles River Press.

Kiefer, Charles, and Peter Senge. 1984. "Metanoic Organizations." In *Transforming Work*, edited by John Adams. Alexandria, Va.: Miles River Press.

Kiefer, Charles, and Peter Stroh. 1984. "A New Paradigm for Developing Organizations." In *Transforming Work*, edited by John Adams. Alexandria, Va.: Miles River Press.

Kitwood, Tom. 1979. "Technology and Justice Viewed from a Third World Context." *Alternative Futures* 2(3): 17–38.

Kleeman, Walter, Jr. 1974. "Humanizing Offices by Participatory Design." In *Humanizing the Workplace*, edited by Roy Fairfield. Buffalo, N.Y.: Prometheus Books.

Koenig, Herman. 1978. "Appropriate Technology and Resources." In *Appropriate Visions*, edited by Richard Dorf and Yvonne Hunter. San Francisco: Boyd & Fraser.

Kotkin, Joel, and Yoriko Kishimoto. 1988. *The Third Century: America's Resurgence in the Asian Era*. New York: Crown.

Kotz, Nick. 1976. "Agribusiness." In *Radical Agriculture*, edited by Richard Merrill. New York: New York University Press.

Kramer, Diane. 1992. "The Urge to Incubate Companies." *The New York Times*, May 3.

Kreman, Bennett. 1974. "Search for a Better Way of Work: Lordstown, Ohio." In *Humanizing the Workplace*, edited by Roy Fairfield. Buffalo, N.Y.: Prometheus Books.

Krieger, Leonard. 1973. "Authority." In *Dictionary of the History of Ideas*, vol.1. New York: Charles Scribner's Sons.

Kuhn, Thomas. 1970. *The Structure of Scientific Revolutions*. 2nd ed. Chicago: University of Chicago Press.

Kurtzman, Joel. 1992. "Business Diary." *The New York Times*, April 19.

Land, George. 1986. *Grow or Die: The Unifying Principle of Transformation*. New York: Wiley.

Land, George, and Beth Jarman. 1992. *Breakpoint and Beyond: Mastering the Future Today*. New York: HarperCollins.

Lao Tzu. 1963. *Tao Te Ching*. Translated by D. C. Lau. New York: Penguin.

Lappé, Frances Moore. 1971. *Diet for a Small Planet*. New York: Ballantine.

Laszlo, Ervin, ed. 1973. *The World System: Models, Norms, Applications*. New York: Braziller.

———. 1976. *Goals for Mankind*. New York: Dutton.

Leipert, Christian. 1986. "From Gross to Adjusted National Product." In *The Living Economy*, edited by Paul Ekins. New York: Routledge & Kegan Paul.

Leonard, George. 1988. *Walking on the Edge of the World*. Boston: Houghton Mifflin.

Leopold, Aldo. 1966. *A Sand County Almanac*. New York: Ballantine.

Levering, Robert. 1988. *A Great Place to Work*. New York: Random House.

Lewis, Paul. 1992. "Fixing World Crises Isn't Just a Job for Diplomats." *The New York Times*, April 5.

Linton, Ron. 1970. *Terracide: America's Destruction of Her Living Environment*. Boston: Little, Brown.

Lohr, Steve. 1992. "Pulling Down the Corporate Clubhouse." *The New York Times*, April 12.

Lovelock, J. E. 1979. *Gaia: A New Look at Life on Earth*. Oxford: Oxford University Press.

Lovins, Amory. 1977. *Soft Energy Paths: Toward a Durable Peace*. San Francisco: Friends of the Earth International.

————. 1978. "Energy Strategy: The Road Not Taken." In *Stepping Stones*, edited by Lane de Moll and Gigi Coe. New York: Schocken.

Lundborg, Louis. 1978. "Changing the Scale of Technology: Paths to the Future." In *Appropriate Visions*, edited by Richard Dorf and Yvonne Hunter. San Francisco: Boyd & Fraser.

Lutz, Mark, and Kenneth Lux. 1979. *The Challenge of Humanistic Economics*. Menlo Park, Calif.: Benjamin-Cummings.

Maccoby, Michael. 1988. *Why Work: Leading the New Generation*. New York: Simon & Schuster.

Macy, Joanna. 1983. *Despair and Personal Power in the Nuclear Age*. Philadelphia: New Society Publishers.

Maranto, Gina. 1992. "Saving Ourselves." *The New York Times*, February 9.

Max-Neff, Manfred. 1986. "Human-Scale Economics: The Challenges Ahead." In *The Living Economy*, edited by Paul Ekins. London: Routledge & Kegan Paul.

McHugh, Paul. 1992. "Reinventing the Map." *San Francisco Chronicle, This World*, September 13, 7–11.

McKean, Roland. 1975. "Economics of Trust, Altruism and Corporate Responsibility." In *Altruism, Morality and Economic Theory*. New York: Russell Sage Foundation.

McKibben, William. 1989. *The End of Nature*. New York: Random House.

McLuhan, Marshall, and Bruce Powers. 1989. *The Global Village: Transformations in World Life and Media in the Twenty-First Century*. New York: Oxford University Press.

McRobie, George. 1977. "An Approach for Appropriate Technologists." In *Appropriate Technology*, edited by R. J. Congdon. Emmaus, Pa.: Rodale Press.

————. 1981. *Small Is Possible*. New York: Harper & Row.

Meador, Roy. 1978. *Future Energy Alternatives: Long-Range Energy Prospects for America and the World*. Ann Arbor, Mich.: Ann Arbor Science.

Meadows, Donella. 1988a. "How Can We Improve Our Chances?" In *The Cassandra Conference*, edited by Paul Ehrlich and John Holdren. College Station: Texas A&M University Press.

————. 1988b. "The Limits to Growth Revisited." In *The Cassandra Conference*, edited by Paul Ehrlich and John Holdren. College Station: Texas A&M University Press.

————, et al. 1974. *The Limits to Growth: A Report for the Club of Rome's Project on the Predicament of Mankind*. New York: Universe Books.

Mehrtens, Susan, and Charles Juzek, eds. 1974. *Earthkeeping: Readings in Human Ecology*. Pacific Grove, Calif.: Boxwood Press.

Merrill, Richard, ed. 1976a. *Radical Agriculture*. New York: New York University Press.

————. 1976b. "Toward a Self-Sustaining Agriculture." In *Radical Agriculture*, edited by Richard Merrill. New York: New York University Press.

Mesarovic, Mihajlo, and Eduard Pestel. 1974. *Mankind at the Turning Point*. New York: Dutton.

Metzner, Ralph. 1986. *Opening to Inner Light: The Transformation of Human Nature and Consciousness*. Los Angeles: Tarcher.

Meyer, Christopher. 1986. "Leadership Can't Be Taught—Only Learned." In *Transforming Leadership*, edited by John Adams. Alexandria, Va.: Miles River Press.

Milenkovitch, D. D. 1975. "The Worker-Managed Enterprise." In *Self-Management*, edited by Jaroslav Vanek. Baltimore: Penguin.

Miller, Thomas. 1988. "31 Major Trends Shaping the Future of American Business." *The Public Pulse*, 2(1).

Miller, William C. 1992. "How Do We Put Our Spiritual Values to Work?" In *New Traditions in Business*, edited by John Renesch. San Francisco: Berrett-Koehler.

Mills, D. Quinn. 1990. *Rebirth of the Corporation*. New York: Wiley.

Mishan, Ezra. 1967. *The Costs of Economic Growth*. New York: Praeger.

————. 1977. *The Economic Growth Debate: An Assessment*. London: Allen & Unwin.

————. 1980. *Pornography, Psychedelics and Technology: Essays on the Limits to Freedom*. London: Allen & Unwin.

Mobley, Lou, and Kate McKeown. 1989. *Beyond IBM: Leadership, Marketing and Finance for the 1990s*. Washington, D.C.: Enter Publishing.

Moelaert, John. 1974. "The Epidemic in Our Midst." In *Earthkeeping*, edited by Susan Mehrtens and Charles Juzek. Pacific Grove, Calif.: Boxwood Press.

Mollner, Terry. 1988. "The Third Way Is Here." *In Context*, Autumn.

Moncrief, Lewis. 1974. "The Cultural Basis for Our Environmental Crisis." In *Ecology and Religion in History*, edited by David Spring and Eileen Spring. New York: Harper & Row.

Morin, William. 1992. "Help for the Post-Layoff 'Survivors'." *The New York Times*, January 5.

Moskowitz, Milton. 1992. "The New Economic Zeitgeist." *Business Ethics*, January/February.

Muller, Robert. 1982. *New Genesis: Shaping a Global Spirituality*. New York: Doubleday.

Murray, Bertram, Jr. 1974. "What the Ecologists Can Teach the Economists." In *Earthkeeping*, edited by Susan Mehrtens and Charles Juzek. Pacific Grove, Calif.: Boxwood Press.

Nader, Ralph. 1970. "Introduction." In *Ecotactics*, edited by John Mitchell. New York: Pocket Books.

Nader, Ralph, Mark Green, and Joel Seligman. 1976. *Taming the Giant Corporation*. New York: Norton.

Naisbitt, John. 1984. *Megatrends*. New York: Warner.

Naisbitt, John, and Patricia Aburdene. 1985. *Reinventing the Corporation*. New York: Warner.

————. 1990. *Megatrends 2000: Ten New Directions for the 1990's*. New York: Avon.

Nasar, Sylvia. 1992. "Fed Gives New Evidence of 80's Gains by Richest." *The New York Times*, April 21.

Natale, Samuel, and John Wilson. 1990. *The Ethical Context for Business Conflicts*. New York: University Press of America.

Nicholson, Max. 1987. *The New Environmental Age*. New York: Cambridge University Press.

Noble, Barbara P. 1992. "Making Family Leave a Local Issue." *The New York Times*, March 22.

Norton, Rob. 1991. "The Most Fascinating Ideas for 1991." *Fortune*, January 14.

"Not Business As Usual." *Business Ethics*, March/April 1992.

Oakeshott, R. 1975. "Mondragon: Spain's Oasis of Democracy." In *Self-Management*, edited by Jaroslav Vanek. Baltimore: Penguin.

Odum, Howard. 1971. *Environment, Power and Society*. New York: Wiley-Interscience.

———. 1978. "Energy, Ecology, and Economics." In *Stepping Stones*, edited by Lane de Moll and Gigi Coe. New York: Schocken.

Ohmae, Kenichi. 1990. *The Borderless World: Power and Strategy in the Interlinked Economy*. New York: Harper & Row.

Ornstein, Robert, and Paul Ehrlich. 1989. *New World, New Mind: Moving Toward Conscious Evolution*. New York: Doubleday.

Orsborn, Carol. 1992. *Inner Excellence: Spiritual Principles of Life-Driven Business*. San Rafael, Calif.: New World Library.

O'Toole, James. 1985. *Vanguard Management*. New York: Doubleday.

Owen, Harrison. 1984. "Facilitating Organizational Transformation: The Use of Myth and Ritual." In *Transforming Work*, edited by John Adams. Alexandria, Va.: Miles River Press.

———. 1986. "Leadership by Indirection." In *Transforming Leadership*, edited by John Adams. Alexandria, Va. Miles River Press.

Pacek, Joze. 1975. "Self-Management: The Experience and the Results." In *Self-Management*, edited by Ichak Adizes and Elisabeth Borgese. Santa Barbara, Calif.: ABC-Clio.

Pascarella, Perry. 1984. *The New Achievers: Creating a Modern Work Ethic*. New York: Macmillan.

———. 1986. "The New Science of Management." *Industry Week*, January 6.

Peck, M. Scott. 1978. *The Road Less Travelled*. New York: Simon & Schuster.

———. 1987. *The Different Drum: Community Making and Peace*. New York: Simon & Schuster.

Pehrson, John B. 1992. "Creative Imaging in Business—A Whole-Brain Approach to Deeper Insight." *World Business Academy Perspectives* 6(1): 27–36.

Pelletier, Kenneth. 1977. *Mind as Healer, Mind as Slayer: A Holistic Approach to Preventing Stress Disorders*. New York: Delta.

———. 1978. *Toward a Science of Consciousness*. New York: Delacorte.

———. 1979. *Holistic Medicine: From Stress to Optimum Health*. New York: Delta/Seymour Lawrence.

Perelman, Michael. 1976. "Efficiency in Agriculture: The Economics of Energy." In *Radical Agriculture*, edited by Richard Merrill. New York: New York University Press.

Pert, Candace. 1987. "Neuropeptides, The Emotions and Bodymind." In *Consciousness and Survival*, edited by J. Spong. Sausalito, Calif.: Institute of Noetic Sciences.

Peters, Thomas, and Robert Waterman, Jr. 1982. *In Search of Excellence: Lessons from America's Best-Run Companies.* New York: Warner.

Petersen, Donald, and John Hillkirk. 1991. *A Better Idea: Redefining the Way Americans Work.* Boston: Houghton Mifflin.

Pitt, D. C. 1988. *The Future of the Environment.* London: Routledge & Kegan Paul.

Pollack, Andrew. 1992. "The Global Lab: Technology Without Borders Raises Big Questions for U.S." *The New York Times*, January 1.

Porter, Maya. n.d. *The Wake-Up Call: Coming to Consciousness.* Potomac, Md.

Powell, Gary. 1988. *Women and Men in Management.* New York: Sage.

Prigogine, Ilya. 1980. *From Being to Becoming: Time and Complexity in the Physical Sciences.* New York: W. H. Freeman.

Purdum, Todd. 1992. "Dedicated Taxes: Good Policy or Bad Planning?" *The New York Times*, April 19.

Rainbook: Resources for Appropriate Technology. New York: Schocken, 1977.

Raver, Ann. 1992. "Farmers Worried as a Chemical Friend Turns Foe." *The New York Times*, February 24.

Ravo, Nick. 1992. "For the '90's, Lavish Amounts of Stinginess." *The New York Times*, January 15.

Ray, Michael, and Rochelle Myers. 1986. *Creativity in Business.* New York: Doubleday.

Reich, Richard. 1990. "Today's Leaders Look at Tomorrow." *Fortune*, March 26.

Renesch, John. 1991. "The End of Knowing It All: A Time for Personal Humility and Organizational Learning in Business." *The New Leaders*, September/October.

———, ed. 1992. *New Traditions in Business: Spirit and Leadership in the 21st Century.* San Francisco: Berrett-Koehler.

Riegel, E. C. 1944. *Private Enterprise Money: A Non-Political Money System.* New York: Harbinger House.

Rifkin, Glenn. 1991. "Do Employees Have a Right to Electronic Privacy?" *The New York Times*, December 8.

———. 1992. "Ardent Preacher of Radical Change." *The New York Times*, April 18.

Rifkin, Jeremy. 1983. *Algeny: A New Word, A New World*. New York: Viking.

Rifkin, Jeremy, with Ted Howard and N. Banks. 1980. *Entropy: A New Worldview*. New York: Viking.

Robertson, James. 1986. "The Mismatch Between Health and Economics." In *The Living Economy*, edited by Paul Ekins. London: Routledge & Kegan Paul.

Robinson, Joan. 1973. *Economic Heresies*. New York: Basic Books.

Rose, Frank. 1990. "A New Age for Business?" *Fortune*, October 8.

Rothschild, Michael. 1991. "Call It Digital Darwinism." *Upside*, December.

Rothstein, Edward. 1992. "In the Fracas Over a Prize, No One Won." *The New York Times*, April 19.

Rothwell, Sheila. 1986. "Flexible Working Patterns." In *The Living Economy*, edited by Paul Ekins. London: Routledge & Kegan Paul.

Rowland, Mary. 1992. "A Farewell to Paternalism." *The New York Times*, March 8.

Russell, Peter. 1983. *The Global Brain: Speculations on the Evolutionary Leap to Planetary Consciousness*. Los Angeles: Tarcher.

Russell, Peter, and Roger Evans. 1992. *The Creative Manager*. San Francisco: Jossey-Bass.

Rybczynski, Witold. 1980. *Paper Heroes: A Review of Appropriate Technology*. New York: Doubleday.

———. 1983. *Taming the Tiger: The Struggle to Control Technology*. New York: Viking.

Sachs, Wolfgang. 1986. "Delinking from the World Market." In *The Living Economy*, edited by Paul Ekins. London: Routledge & Kegan Paul.

Sale, Kirkpatrick. 1980. *Human Scale*. New York: Coward, McCann & Geohegan.

———. 1986. "Dwellers in the Land: The Bioregional Vision." *Utne Reader*, February/March.

Sanger, David. 1992a. "As Ugly Feelings Grow, It's Hard to Separate Fact and Fiction." *The New York Times*, January 26.

———. 1992b. "The Dominoes That Didn't Fall." *The New York Times Book Review*, January 19.

Satin, Mark. 1979. *New Age Politics: Healing Self and Society*. New York: Delta.

Schaef, Anne Wilson. 1985. *Women's Reality: An Emerging Female System in a White Male Society*. New York: Harper & Row.

———. 1986. *Co-Dependence: Misunderstood, Mistreated*. New York: Harper & Row.

Schaef, Anne Wilson, and Diane Fassel. 1988. *The Addictive Organization*. New York: Harper & Row.

Schatz, Joel, and Tom Bender. 1978. "Cosmic Economics." In *Stepping Stones*, edited by Lane de Moll and Gigi Coe. New York: Schocken.

Schmidheiny, Stephan, with the Business Council for Sustainable Development. 1992. *Changing Course: A Global Business Perspective on Development and the Environment*. Cambridge, Mass.: MIT Press.

Schonberger, Richard. 1974. "Toward a Greater Flexibility." In *Humanizing the Workplace*, edited by Roy Fairfield. Buffalo, N.Y.: Prometheus Books.

Schrank, Robert. 1974. "On Ending Worker Alienation: The Gaines Pet Food Plant." In *Humanizing the Workplace*, edited by Roy Fairfield. Buffalo, N.Y.: Prometheus Books.

Schumacher, E. F. 1973a. "Buddhist Economics." In *Toward a Steady-State Economy*, edited by Herman Daly. San Francisco: W. H. Freeman.

———. 1973b. *Small Is Beautiful: Economics As If People Mattered*. New York: Harper & Row.

———. 1978a. "Automation and the Scale of Technology." In *Appropriate Visions*, edited by Richard Dorf and Yvonne Hunter. San Francisco: Boyd & Fraser.

———. 1978b. "Conscious Culture of Poverty." In *Stepping Stones*, edited by Lane de Moll and Gigi Coe. New York: Schocken.

———. 1978c. "The Ethics of Thinking Small." In *Appropriate Visions*, edited by Richard Dorf and Yvonne Hunter. San Francisco: Boyd & Fraser.

———. 1978d. *A Guide for the Perplexed*. New York: Harper & Row.

———. 1978e. "Intermediate Technology and the Individual." In *Appropriate Visions*, edited by Richard Dorf and Yvonne Hunter. San Francisco: Boyd & Fraser.

———. 1978f. "Time to Stop." In *Stepping Stones*, edited by Lane de Moll and Gigi Coe. New York: Schocken.

————. 1979. *Good Work*. New York: Harper & Row.

Schwartz, Peter, and James Ogilvy. 1979. *The Emergent Paradigm: Changing Patterns of Thought and Belief*. Menlo Park, Calif.: SRI International Values and Lifestyles Program.

Sculley, John. 1987. *Odyssey: From Pepsi to Apple*. New York: Simon & Schuster.

Sears, Paul. 1969. "The Steady State: Physical Law and Moral Choice." In *The Subversive Science*, edited by Paul Shepard and Daniel McKinley. Boston: Houghton Mifflin.

"Seize the Future." *Success*, March 1990.

Senge, Peter. 1986. "Systems Principles for Leadership." In *Transforming Leadership*, edited by John Adams. Alexandria, Va.: Miles River Press.

————. 1990. *The Fifth Discipline: The Art and Practice of the Learning Organization*. New York: Doubleday.

Shames, Richard, and Chuck Sterin. 1978. *Healing with Mind Power*. Emmaus, Pa.: Rodale Press.

Shepard, Paul, and Daniel McKinley, eds. 1969. *The Subversive Science: Essays Toward an Ecology of Man*. Boston: Houghton Mifflin.

Sibbet, David, and Juanita Brown. 1986. "Leading as Learning: Developing a Community's Foundation." In *Transforming Leadership*, edited by John Adams. Alexandria, Va.: Miles River Press.

Siegel, Bernard. 1985. "A Yale Surgeon Says Cancer Has a Positive Message for Humanity." *The Tarrytown Letter*, no. 46.

Simons, Marlise. 1992. "Ecological Plea from Executives." *The New York Times*, May 8.

"Some Lines on the Rest of the Millenium." *The New York Times*, December 24, 1989.

Speck, Frank. 1935. *The Naskapi: The Savage Hunter of the Labrador Peninsula*. Norman: University of Oklahoma Press.

Sperry, R. W. 1978. "Mentalist Monism: Consciousness as a Causal Emergent of Brain Processes." *Behavioral & Brain Sciences* 3, 365–367.

Spretnak, Charlene, and Fritjof Capra. 1986. *Green Politics*. Santa Fe, N. Mex.: Bear & Co.

Steele, Shelby. 1990. "A Negative Vote on Affirmative Action." *The New York Times*, May 13.

Stein, Barry. 1978. "Small Business: Testimony to the Senate Small Business Committee." In *Stepping Stones*, edited by Lane de Moll and Gigi Coe. New York: Schocken.

Stein, Murray. 1990. "The Spirit of Transformation in Corporate Life." *Psychological Perspectives* 22.

Steinfels, Peter. 1992. "Beliefs." *The New York Times*, April 25.

Stevenson, Richard. 1992. "Monitoring Pollution at Its Source." *The New York Times*, April 8.

Storer, Jon. 1956. *The Web of Life: A First Book of Ecology*. New York: New American Library.

———. 1968. *Man in the Web of Life*. New York: New American Library.

Stroh, Linda, Anne Reilly, and Jeanne Brett. 1990. "New Trends in Relocation." *HR Magazine*, February.

Strom, Stephanie. 1992a. "In the Gray 90's, Women Are Heading Back to the Bobbin." *The New York Times*, March 29.

———. 1992b. "More Suppliers Helping Stores Push the Goods." *The New York Times*, January 20.

———. 1992c. "Playing as a Team" *The New York Times Book Review*, January 5.

Swazy, Alecia. 1991. "Changing Times." *Wall Street Journal*, March 22.

Swimme, Brian. 1984. *The Universe Is a Green Dragon: A Cosmic Creation Story*. Santa Fe, N. Mex.: Bear & Co.

Tart, Charles. 1987. *Waking Up: Overcoming the Obstacles to Human Potential*. Boston: Shambhala.

Theobald, Robert. 1987. *The Rapids of Change: Social Entrepreneurship in Turbulent Times*. Indianapolis, Ind.: Knowledge Systems.

Thorsrud, Einar, and Fred Emery. 1975. "Industrial Democracy in Norway: Employee Representation and Personal Participation." In *Self-Management*, edited by Ichak Adizes & Elisabeth Borgese. Santa Barbara, Calif.: ABC-Clio.

Thurow, Lester. 1990. "Global Trade: The Secrets of Success." *The New York Times Book Review*, May 27.

Tinbergen, Jan. 1976. *Reshaping the International Order: A Report to the Club of Rome*. New York: Dutton.

"Today's Leaders Look at Tomorrow." *Fortune*, March 26, 1990.

Todd, John. 1976. "A Modern Proposal: Science for the People." In *Radical Agriculture*, edited by Richard Merrill. New York: New York University Press.

Todd, John, and Nancy Todd. 1980. *Tomorrow Is Our Permanent Address*. New York: Harper & Row.

Toffler, Alvin. 1975. *The Eco-Spasm Report*. New York: Bantam.

———. 1980. *The Third Wave*. New York: Morrow.

———. 1990. *Powershift*. New York: Bantam.

Trefel, James. 1992. "A Picture Is Worth a Zillion Bits." *The New York Times*, April 9.

Turner, Thomas. 1970. "Eco-Pornography or How to Spot an Ecological Phony." In *The Environmental Handbook*, edited by Garrett de Bell. New York: Ballantine.

Valashakis, Kimon, Peter Sidall, S. Graham Smith, and Iris Fitzpatrick-Martin. 1979. *The Conserver Society: A Workable Alternative for the Future*. New York: Harper & Row.

Van der Ryn, Sim. 1978a. "What Is Appropriate Technology?" In *Appropriate Visions*, edited by Richard Dorf and Yvonne Hunter. San Francisco: Boyd & Fraser.

———. 1978b. "Working with and Through Institutions." In *Appropriate Visions*, edited by Richard Dorf and Yvonne Hunter. San Francisco: Boyd & Fraser.

Vanek, Jaroslav. 1975a. "The Basic Theory of Financing of Participatory Firms." In *Self-Management*, edited by Jaroslav Vanek. Baltimore: Penguin.

———. 1975b. "Decentralization Under Workers' Management: A Theoretical Appraisal." In *Self-Management*, edited by Jaroslav Vanek. Baltimore: Penguin.

———, ed. 1975c. *Self-Management: Economic Liberation of Man*. Baltimore: Penguin.

———. 1975d. "The Worker-Managed Enterprise as an Institution." In *Self-Management*, edited by Jaroslav Vanek. Baltimore: Penguin.

Vaughn, Frances. 1979. *Awakening Intuition*. New York: Doubleday.

Vickers, Geoffrey. 1970. *Freedom in a Rocking Boat: Changing Values in an Unstable Society*. Baltimore: Penguin.

Vogel, Ezra. 1991. *The Four Little Dragons: The Spread of Industrialization in East Asia*. Cambridge, Mass.: Harvard University Press.

von Franz, Marie Louise. 1964. "The Process of Individuation." In *Man and His Symbols*, edited by C. G. Jung, M. L. von Franz, J. Henderson, J. Jacobs, and A. Jaffé. New York: Dell.

Wallich, Franklin. 1974. "Work with Dignity." In *Humanizing the Workplace*, edited by Roy Fairfield. Buffalo, N.Y.: Prometheus Books.

Walsh, Roger. 1983. "The Consciousness Disciplines." *Journal of Humanistic Psychology* 23(2): 28–30.

Weiss, Rich. 1992. "Travel Can Be Sickening; Now Scientists Know Why." *The New York Times*, April 28.

Welsh, Patrick. 1990. "Why Our Students Keep Snoozing Through Science." *The Washington Post*, May 20.

White, Mary, and Dorothy Van Soest. 1984. *Empowerment of People for Peace*. Minneapolis, Minn.: Women Against Military Madness.

Whitney, Dan. 1978. "Nuclear Energy: An Appropriate Technology?" In *Appropriate Visions*, edited by Richard Dorf and Yvonne Hunter. San Francisco: Boyd & Fraser.

Wigner, Eugene. 1967. "Explaining Consciousness." *Science* 156.

———. 1982. "Conference Speech." In *Mind in Nature: Nobel Conference XVII*, edited by Richard Elvee. New York: Harper & Row.

Winner, Langdon. 1977. *Autonomous Technology*. Cambridge, Mass.: MIT Press.

Woodward, Harry, and Steven Buchholz. 1987. *Aftershock*. New York: Wiley.

World Commission on Environment and Development. 1987. *Our Common Future*. New York: Oxford University Press.

Wright, Robin. 1992. "As World Turns: Experts Foresee 300-Plus Countries." *The Denver Post*, August 30, 19A, 23A.

Wriston, Walter. 1990. "The Refrigerator's Revolutionary Role." *Fortune*, March 26.

Wycliff, Don. 1990. "Blacks Debate the Costs of Affirmative Action." *The New York Times*, June 10.

Yankelovich, Daniel, and Joel Gurin. 1989. "American Dream." *American Health*, March.

Yatri. 1988. *Unknown Man: The Mysterious Birth of a New Species*. New York: Simon & Schuster.

Yudin, Yehuda. 1975. "Industrial Democracy as a Component in Social Change: The Israeli Approach and Experience." In *Self-Management*, edited by Ichak Adizes and Elisabeth Borgese. Santa Barbara, Calif.: ABC-Clio.

Zuboff, Shoshana. 1988. *In the Age of the Smart Machine: The Future of Work and Power*. New York: Basic Books.

Zukav, Gary. 1979. *The Dancing Wu Li Masters: An Overview of the New Physics*. New York: Bantam.

———. 1989. *The Seat of the Soul*. New York: Simon & Schuster.

Zwerdling, Daniel. 1980. *Workplace Democracy: A Guide to Workplace Ownership, Participation and Self-Management Experiments in the United States*. New York: Harper & Row.

Index

Berrett-Koehler Publishers

ERRETT-KOEHLER is an independent publisher of books, periodicals, and other publications at the leading edge of new thinking and innovative practice on work, business, management, leadership, stewardship, career development, human resources, entrepreneurship, and global sustainability.

Since the company's founding in 1992, we have been committed to supporting the movement toward a more enlightened world of work by publishing books, periodicals, and other publications that help us to integrate our values with our work and work lives, and to create more humane and effective organizations.

We have chosen to focus on the areas of work, business, and organizations, because these are central elements in many people's lives today. Furthermore, the work world is going through tumultuous changes, from the decline of job security to the rise of new structures for organizing people and work. We believe that change is needed at all levels—individual, organizational, community, and global—and our publications address each of these levels.

We seek to create new lenses for understanding organizations, to legitimize topics that people care deeply about but that current business orthodoxy censors or considers secondary to bottom-line concerns, and to uncover new meaning, means, and ends for our work and work lives.

See next page for other books from Berrett-Koehler Publishers

Other leading-edge business books
from Berrett-Koehler Publishers

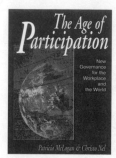

The Age of Participation
New Governance for the Workplace and the World
by Patricia McLagan and Christo Nel
foreword by Peter Block

ATRICIA McLAGAN and Christo Nel describe the massive transformation that is occurring in human institutions today. Blending theory and practice, providing numerous examples, and drawing on more than forty years of experience in over 200 organizations, McLagan and Nel describe what executives, managers, workers, labor unions, customers, and suppliers can do as part of a participative enterprise. In this practical, experience-based handbook, they look closely at every level of life in a participative organization and deflate the fears and misperceptions that can sabotage change.

Hardcover, 300 pages, 9/95 • ISBN 1-881052-56-7 CIP • **Item no. 52567-153 $27.95**

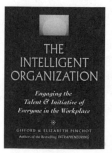

The New Management
Democracy and Enterprise Are Transforming Organizations
William E. Halal

ODAY'S MANAGERS are confronted with a bewildering blur of change, ranging from downsizing to spirituality. *The New Management* cuts through the confusion by integrating emerging practices into a coherent, clarifying whole. Drawing on hundreds of examples from progressive companies, an international survey of 426 managers, and economic trends, William Halal shows how enterprise and democracy are moving inside of business and government to transform institutions for the Information Age.

Hardcover, 300 pages, 5/96 • ISBN 1-881052-53-2 CIP • **Item no. 52532-153 $29.95**

The Intelligent Organization*
Engaging the Talent and Initiative of Everyone in the Workplace
Gifford and Elizabeth Pinchot

HIS BOOK shows how to replace bureaucracy with more humane and effective systems for organizing and coordinating work. Gifford and Elizabeth Pinchot show how, by developing and engaging the intelligence, business judgment, and wide-system responsibility of all its members, an organization can respond more effectively to customers, partners, and competitors.

*Originally published in hardcover with the title *The End of Bureaucracy and the Rise of the Intelligent Organization*

Paperback, 420 pages, 10/96 • ISBN 1-881052-98-2 CIP • **Item no. 52982-153 $19.95**
Hardcover, 3/94 • ISBN 1-881052-34-6 CIP • **Item no. 52346-153 $24.95**

Available at your favorite bookstore, or call 1-800-929-2929

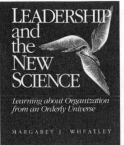

Learning about Organization from an Orderly Universe
Margaret J. Wheatley

"The Best Management Book of the Year!"
—*Industry Week* magazine survey by Tom Brown

OUR UNDERSTANDING of the universe is being radically altered by the "New Science"—the revolutionary discoveries in quantum physics, chaos theory, and evolutionary biology that are overturning the models of science that have dominated for centuries. Now, in this pioneering book, Wheatley shows how the new science provides equally powerful insights for changing how we design, lead, manage, and view organizations.

Paperback, 172 pages, 3/94 • ISBN 1-881052-44-3 CIP • **Item no. 52443-153 $15.95**
Hardcover, 9/92 • ISBN 1-881052-01-X CIP • **Item no. 5201X-153 $24.95**

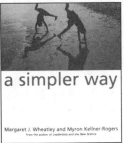

A Simpler Way
Margaret J. Wheatley and Myron Kellner-Rogers

A *SIMPLER WAY* is the widely awaited new book from Margaret J. Wheatley, author of the bestselling *Leadership and the New Science.* Here, Wheatley and coauthor Myron Kellner-Rogers explore the primary question, "How could we organize human endeavor if we developed different understandings of how life organizes itself?" They draw on the work of scientists, philosophers, poets, novelists, spiritual teachers, colleagues, audiences, and each other in search of new ways of understanding life and how organizing activities occur. *A Simpler Way* presents a profoundly different world view that changes how we live our lives and how we can create organizations that thrive.

Hardcover, 168 pages, 9/96 • ISBN 1-881052-95-8 • **Item no. 52958-153 $27.95**

Stewardship
Choosing Service Over Self-Interest
Peter Block

Peter Block shows how to recreate our workplaces by replacing self-interest, dependency, and control with service, responsibility, and partnership. In this revolutionary book, he demonstrates how a far-reaching redistribution of power, privilege, and wealth will radically change all areas of organizational governance, and shows why this is our best hope to enable democracy to thrive, our spiritual and ethical values to be lived out, and economic success to be sustained.

Paperback, 288 pages, 3/96 • ISBN 1-881052-86-9 CIP • **Item no. 52869-153 $16.95**
Hardcover, 7/93 • ISBN 1-881052-28-1 CIP • **Item no. 52281-153 $27.95**

Available at your favorite bookstore, or call 1-800-929-2929

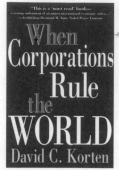

When Corporations Rule the World

–David C. Korten

DAVID KORTEN offers an alarming exposé of the devastating consequences of economic globalization and a passionate message of hope in this well-reasoned, extensively researched analysis. He documents the human and environmental consequences of economic globalization, and explains why human survival depends on a community-based, people-centered alternative. Literate and authoritative, this book is insightful reading for business people, activists, and ordinary citizens who want to restore the balance of power in the world.

Paperback, 384 pages, 9/96 • ISBN 1-887208-01-1 CIP
Item no. 0801-153 $19.95
Hardcover, 9/95 • ISBN 1-887208-00-3 CIP • **Item no. 08003-153 $29.95**

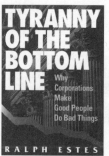

Tyranny of the Bottom Line

Why Corporations Make Good People Do Bad Things

Ralph Estes

HERE IS the story of corporate power gone awry—bringing injury and death to employees, financial and personal loss to customers, desolation to communities, pollution and hazardous waste to the nation. Emphasizing the notion that all of us are stakeholders in the large corporation—with an investment, an interest in its performance, and a right to accountability—Ralph Estes provides a practical, specific plan for creating more effective and humane companies, restoring the original public purpose of the corporate system, and allowing managers to make choices that effectively and ethically balance the interests of everyone.

Hardcover, 310 pages, 1/96 • ISBN 1-881052-75-3 CIP • **Item no. 52753-153 $27.95**

Economic Insanity

How Growth-Driven Capitalism Is Devouring the American Dream

by Roger Terry

THIS PROVOCATIVE book questions the basic assumptions that drive our economic system: endless economic growth, ever-increasing productivity, accelerating technological advances, unfettered competition, and corporate self-interest. Roger Terry shows how these assumptions are causing a host of interrelated and deeply entrenched problems, including the loss of personal freedom and democracy, the perpetual and unavoidable increase in inequality, and the disuniting of America. Incorporating ideas from Adam Smith and Thomas Paine to Paul Johnson and Herman Daly, *Economic Insanity* challenges readers to stop looking for answers within the system and look instead to changing the system.

Hardcover, 200 pages, 10/95 • ISBN 1-881052-32-X CIP • **Item no. 5232X-153 $24.95**

Available at your favorite bookstore, or call 1-800-929-2929